GL●BAL PROFILES

CONTEMPORARY HUMAN RIGHTS ACTIVISTS

Eileen Lucas

☑® Facts On File, Inc.

Contemporary Human Rights Activists

Facts On File, Inc.
11 Penn Plaza
New York NY 10001

Library of Congress Cataloging-in-Publication Data

Lucas, Eileen.
    Contemporary human rights activists / Eileen Lucas.
        p.   cm. — (Global profiles)
    Includes bibliographical references and index.
    Summary: Profiles ten significant figures in the world-wide
  struggle for human rights, including Mother Teresa, Archbishop
  Desmond Tutu, Joan Baez, Jimmy Carter, and Fang Lizhi.
    ISBN 0-8160-3298-X
    1. Human rights workers—Biography—Juvenile literature.
  [1. Human rights workers.]   I. Title.   II. Series.
  JC571.L83   1997
  323'.092'2—dc20   96-41253
  [B]

Facts On File books are available at special discounts when purchased in bulk quantities for businesses, associations, institutions or sales promotions. Please call our Special Sales Department in New York at (212) 967–8800 or (800) 322–8755.

Text design by Cathy Rincon
Cover design by Nora Wertz

Printed in the United States of America

MP FOF 10 9 8 7 6 5 4 3 2 1

This book is printed on acid-free paper.

Contents

Introduction

In a stately hotel meeting room in Vienna, Austria, diplomats from around the world listened to distinguished speakers talk about human rights. On the streets outside the hotel, members of an international human rights organization handed out pamphlets and passed around petitions as part of a campaign to stop torture. In a house on a busy street in Rangoon, Burma (now Myanmar), a woman was under house arrest. In a poor section of Mexico City, a Guatemalan refugee dared not leave her home alone because she had received numerous threats against her life.

In mid-June 1993, all these things happened. All involved the struggle for human rights. This struggle has gone on for a long time, and will continue as long as governments deny citizens their rights as human beings.

That's what human rights are all about—the rights that individuals have simply by virtue of being human. These include basics such as the right to remain alive and unharmed, access to food and shelter, the ability to move freely from place to place, and to express one's thoughts and feelings.

The modern human rights movement rose from the rubble of World War II. The deliberate and systematic murder of millions of Jews and other innocent civilians by the Nazis, and the terrible loss of life as a result of military action during that conflict, spurred many of the world's leaders to look for a way to prevent such horrors from happening ever again. Out of this concern the United Nations was founded to provide an organization in which the nations of the world could work together toward a more peaceful future. Fifty nations signed the U.N. Charter in October 1945.

The introduction to the U.N. Charter declares that the members of the United Nations should "reaffirm faith in fundamental human rights, in the dignity and worth of the human person, in the equal rights of men and women and of nations large and small." As one of the principal purposes of the organization, Article 1 lists "encouraging respect for human rights and for fundamental freedoms for all."

Some of the leaders involved wanted more. They established a commission to create something more specific, an "International Bill of Rights." The General Assembly of the United Nations adopted The Universal Declaration of Human Rights on December 10, 1948, a day thereafter commemorated as Human Rights Day. On December 16, 1966, the General Assembly adopted the Covenant on Civil and Political Rights, and the Covenant on Economic, Social, and Cultural Rights. Together these three documents—The Universal Declaration of Human Rights and the two Covenants—make up the International Bill of Rights.

These documents have had a great impact on the way the world views human rights. They give nations a set of standards against which to measure themselves and bind fellow nations. Together with other international agreements that cover human rights, such as the European Convention on Human Rights, the Helsinki Accords, and others, they give human rights activists tools to use in championing human rights.

Because there is all too often a huge gap between the commitments nations make and what they actually do, increasing attention has been paid in the last several decades to the people who fight for human rights. Since 1960 over a dozen human rights activists have won Nobel Peace Prizes, a clear indication of the connection between the quests for peace and human rights. As author Irwin Abrams writes in his book on the Peace Prize, "This conception is in keeping with that of peace scholars today, who do not think of peace as concerned only with relations between states or as merely the absence of war. There is no real peace, they point out, where the enforcement of the status quo involves the suppression of individual freedoms."

Who are human rights activists? This book takes a look at the lives and the work of a few. Born in the Balkan mountains of southeastern Europe, Mother Teresa went to India as a Catholic missionary. Her calling there, among some of the poorest people of the world, was to work to alleviate their misery. In the midst of great suffering, she sees only the opportunity to serve her God by caring for people.

One of the organizations that works for human rights around the world is Amnesty International. Amnesty was started in 1961 by an Englishman named Peter Benenson who not only wanted to *do* something about human rights, but wanted to get other people involved as well.

In 1977, Jimmy Carter became president of the United States and went further than any other president in using the power and prestige of that office to champion human rights. After leaving the presidency, he discovered that he still had access to many valuable resources, and he has continued to use those resources responsibly for the betterment of humanity.

"I detest your views, but I am prepared to die for your right to express them."

—attributed to Voltaire, quoted in *A Flame in Barbed Wire*

Archbishop Desmond Tutu became an Anglican priest in South Africa when his country's racist policies closed off most other careers of service. He rose to the highest position in his church in his country, arguing passionately for justice for all South African people.

The Argentine Mothers of the Plaza de Mayo, led by Hebe de Bonafini and María Adela de Antokoletz, cried out for justice. Their government had launched a so-called Dirty War against "subversives" that trampled the rights of all Argentines and cost thousands of lives. The Mothers gathered, and continue to gather, to demand information about their children who "disappeared" into the dark world of Argentine prisons and torture chambers.

Fang Lizhi of China (now living in exile in the United States), and Aung San Suu Kyi of Burma are both scholars and teachers whose desire to seek and speak the truth thrust them into the heart of democracy movements in their respective countries. When their governments responded to the call for freedom with brutality, each paid a heavy personal price.

Joan Baez is known to many as a folksinger, but to those who look closer she is a singer with something very important to say. Combining music with a message of peace and nonviolence, Baez participates in the human rights movement in the United States and has supported the efforts of human rights activists around the world, including many of the individuals profiled here.

> "The hope for humanity lies with the millions of men and women who have committed themselves in one way or another to defending human rights. We must do all we can to protect them now and keep them alive."
>
> —Amnesty International, 1994 *Report on Human Rights Around the World*

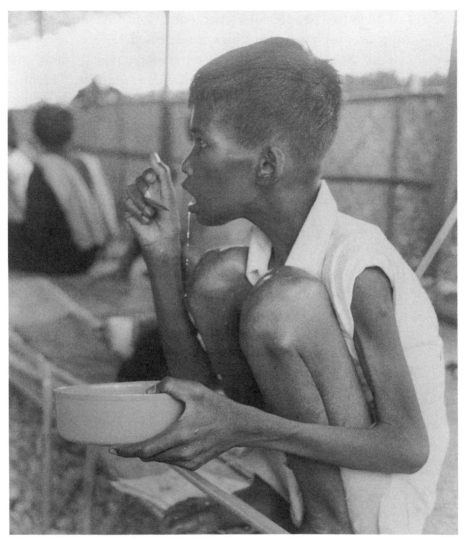

All over the world, countless numbers of people are forced to flee from their homes and perhaps even their country because of war. The plight of such refugees is a major human rights concern. (Courtesy Jimmy Carter Library)

Rigoberta Menchú knows what it's like to live in a land where the government is an enemy: both her parents met violent ends at the hands of military forces. Now she fights for the right of her people, the Maya Indians of Guatemala, and all native peoples of Central and South America, to live in peace, and have their culture respected.

This book is limited to current activists: there are many—Albert Schweitzer, Mohandas Gandhi, Eleanor Roosevelt, Martin Luther King, Jr.—on whose work these activists have built. The book is also limited by space. Many others could have been included; their stories will have to be told some other time and place: Elie Wiesel, Holocaust survivor, and Tenzin Gyatso, exiled Tibetan religious and civil leader, come immediately to mind. It is hoped that the stories told here will encourage you to learn more about these people and others, and to *do* something too.

Further Reading

Abrams, Irwin. *The Nobel Peace Prize and the Laureates*. Boston: G.K. Hall and Co., 1988. A biographical history of the peace prize and the people who won it between 1901 and 1987.

Amnesty International. *The 1994 Report on Human Rights Around the World*. Alameda, Calif.: Hunter House, 1994. Each year Amnesty International publishes this report on the human rights records of the various nations and regions of the world.

Drinan, Robert F. *Cry of the Oppressed, The History and Hope of the Human Rights Revolution*. San Francisco, Calif.: Harper and Row, 1987. An overview of the modern human rights movement, including the founding of the United Nations, the creation of Amnesty International, and the work of other organizations and individuals.

Humphrey, John P. *Human Rights and the United Nations: A Great Adventure*. Dobbs Ferry, N.Y.: Transnational Publishers, Inc., 1984. Humphrey was the first director of the United

Nations Division of Human Rights. This is his account of that work.

Kronenwetter, Michael. *Taking a Stand Against Human Rights Abuses*. New York: Franklin Watts, 1990. A discussion and examination of governments that abuse human rights. Written for young adults.

Selby, David. *Human Rights*. Cambridge, England: Cambridge University Press, 1987. An excellent overview of international human rights issues.

Mother Teresa has struggled to help the "poorest of the poor" in India and around the world since 1948. (Courtesy Bettmann Archives)

Mother Teresa

TOUCHING THE POOR OF INDIA AND THE WORLD (1910–)

A small woman sat on a train bound for Darjeeling, India, deep in thought. She wore the black habit and white head covering of a Roman Catholic nun. As the principal of St. Mary's School in Entally, a small district in the city of Calcutta, she seldom left the peaceful convent grounds except for an emergency, or a retreat, as she was taking now.

As Sister Teresa sat on the train that day, September 10, 1946, however, she was not thinking of the beautiful, peaceful convent. She was thinking of the filthy streets of the *bustees*, or slums, of Calcutta, where the cruelest poverty and violence were the accepted norm. Very clearly, deep within her, Sister Teresa believed that God was telling her to go there, to the *bustees*, to serve "the poorest of the poor." She did not believe she was being called to leave her vocation as a nun, but to take that vocation a step further. She described the experience as "a call within a call." Her followers, who would one day number in the thousands and work among the poor around the world, would celebrate September 10, 1946 as "Inspiration Day." It was the beginning of one of the greatest charitable efforts ever made by a single human being.

The road to India began in a small town, Skopje, in the Balkan mountains of what is now Serbia. There, on August 27, 1910, a baby girl was born to Albanian parents. Christened Agnes Gonxha Bojaxhiu, she was the youngest of three children in what she later described as a happy family. Her father was a merchant who traveled often, buying and selling goods. Her mother was a devout Catholic. Agnes often attended daily mass with her and brought food and clothing to the poor in the area. When her father died in 1918, Agnes' mother struggled to make ends meet, but still they continued to help those even more needy than themselves. As biographer David Porter writes, "Agnes received her first lessons in caring—her first missionary training—in the environment of her family home."

By the time she was 18, Agnes decided to become a missionary. More than anything, she wanted to go to India. She heard the stories of Yugoslavian priests who worked in India, and the many needs of the people there. On September 25, 1928, she left her home and family and traveled by train across Europe and then by ship to Dublin, Ireland. In Dublin the Sisters of Loreto, an order of nuns who serve in India, had their motherhouse. Here Agnes learned English, the language of the order, and began her training as a nun.

On December 1, 1928, Agnes was on her way to India, arriving on January 6, 1929. At the Loreto Convent in Darjeeling, in the foothills of the Himalayas, she continued her studies to become a nun, and taught in the convent school. She also helped in the hospital, where she cared for people covered in sores from their ears to their feet and suffering from fevers. She took the name of Teresa, after a French nun (St. Thérèse [Teresa] of Lisieux) who had sought to serve God in a "little way," by doing menial work cheerfully.

After some time Sister Teresa, as Agnes was now known, was sent to Calcutta, where she taught at St. Mary's school. In May 1937, she took her final vows. Shortly thereafter she became principal of St. Mary's. Over the next decade, she continued to teach there and at St. Teresa's, a short walk through the slum neighborhood outside the convent walls.

In August 1946, there was an outbreak of horrendous rioting in India, during which more than 4,000 people were killed. Muslims and Hindus were fighting for control of various parts of newly independent India. Streets were literally clogged with the bodies of the dead and dying, as smoke drifted up from the burning buildings and vultures hovered over the carnage. Sister Teresa witnessed the suffering when she had to leave the safety of the convent in order to find food for the girls of her school.

A few weeks later, as she was going to a retreat in Darjeeling, she was inspired to go out among the poor. She grew more certain every day that this was what God wanted her to do, even as she waited a year and prayed about it, as instructed by the archbishop of Calcutta.

Finally, in July 1948, she received permission to leave the convent, though she would remain a nun and abide by her vows of chastity, poverty, and obedience. For one year she could try to prove that there was a mission for her as a nun outside the convent in Calcutta. Sister Teresa was 38 years old and had lived in the convent for nearly 20 years. Leaving was very hard, and it was only her conviction that it was God's will that made her departure possible.

Dressed in a simple sari of cheap white cotton with a border of blue stripes and a cross pinned at the

"Today, talking about the poor is in fashion. Knowing, loving, and serving the poor is quite a different matter."

—Mother Teresa

shoulder, Sister Teresa left the convent on August 16, 1948. First, she traveled 240 miles from Calcutta to a medical mission in Patna, where she learned a great deal about caring for the poor. She also got some very good advice about caring for herself. In her eagerness to share the poverty of the people she would help, Sister Teresa found that she was tempted to go without food. The sisters at the medical mission cautioned her that she would be unable to help anyone if she did not eat sensibly and adequately. Sister Teresa did not forget this lesson and would later share it with her followers—they must eat no more, but also no less, than required for their health.

With gifts of sturdy sandals and much valuable knowledge, Sister Teresa left Patna in December 1948 and returned to Calcutta. Refugees from the civil strife in India were everywhere and conditions were atrocious. She walked through the streets of a slum neighborhood called Motijhil until she found some useful space. She gathered a few children in the courtyard behind some huts and began to teach them the alphabet by writing the letters in the dirt with a stick. Slowly, more children came, and someone brought a little table; from somewhere else came a chair.

When a man named Michael Gomes heard about the little nun living among the poor, he offered her the second floor of his house for her work. It became known as the "house on Creek Lane." Soon she was joined by Subhasini Das, a former student, who chose to give up a comfortable life with her wealthy family to work with Sister Teresa. Subhasini became the first sister of the Congregation of the Missionaries of Charity, the order that Sister Teresa founded. She took the name of Sister Agnes, choosing Sister Teresa's original name.

Sister Teresa and Subhasini were soon joined by Magdalena, another former student, who became Sister Gertrude. As more came, they dressed in simple white saris and joined the work among the poor in the *bustees*. They took care of children and old people, and the sick and dying in the streets. Along with Sister Teresa they begged for food for the hungry; they went into filthy huts and cleaned them. Sister Teresa never asked her assistants to do anything she wouldn't do, but there was nothing Sister Teresa considered herself above doing. All tasks were done with cheerfulness and love.

At the end of one year, the archbishop evaluated the work of Sister Teresa, who had become an Indian citizen. In addition to Sister Teresa's vows of poverty, chastity, and obedience, she added, "to give wholehearted and free service to the poorest of the poor." On October 7, 1950, the Missionaries of Charity were recognized as an official order of the church. As founder of this order, Sister Teresa was recognized as Mother Teresa.

More women joined the work, and within two years they outgrew their house on Creek Lane. The home they found at 54A Lower Circular Road was made available to them by a Muslim man. It became the motherhouse of this Catholic order of nuns.

One day in 1954, Mother Teresa found a woman lying in the street who was so sick and dirty that insects and rodents had already begun to pick at her. Mother Teresa picked the woman up in her arms and carried her to the nearest hospital; the hospital did not want to take this woman who was obviously impoverished and dying. Mother Teresa would not leave, and finally the hospital gave

"'What can I do to help?' Just begin, one, one, one. Begin at home by saying something good to your child, to your husband, to your wife. Begin by helping someone in need in your community, at work or at school. Begin by making whatever you do something beautiful for God."

—Mother Teresa

the woman a bed in which to die. Mother Teresa had known the woman's life could not be saved, but said, "We cannot let a child of God die like an animal in the gutter."

Because Mother Teresa spoke of everyone's God (not just the God of Catholics, but of Hindus, Muslims, and all other religions), she found a place that had been a shelter for pilgrims to the Temple of Kali (a Hindu goddess), and turned it into a hospice for the abandoned dying. It was called Nirmal Hriday, Place of the Pure Hearts. Here the sisters gently and tenderly washed wounds, spoon-fed weak and helpless people, and allowed them to die with dignity. Mother Teresa wanted very much for these people who had "lived like animals to die like people."

Some of the people who died at Nirmal Hriday left young children behind as orphans. Sometimes the sisters found babies abandoned in trash heaps as they traveled around Calcutta. Other children were brought to them by police, or priests, or by parents who couldn't care for them. Mother Teresa and the sisters loved and cared for all the children. A building was rented and furnished, and Shishu Bhavan became a home for these children.

Some of the babies were so tiny or sick that they did not live long. Mother Teresa saw to it that they were held and loved, at least for a few hours of their lives. Many others were able to respond to nourishment and the nurturing of the sisters and survive and grow. Most of these babies would be adopted into homes where they would have the opportunity to live good lives.

In working among the poor of Calcutta, the sisters found that the lepers were often the worst off. Leprosy is a painful, destructive disease that often resulted in making lepers poor, homeless, and lonely, as well as sick. All too often no one else would help, which made Mother Teresa want to help them all the more. In 1957, there were approximately 30,000 lepers in Calcutta.

Mother Teresa has received the Nobel Peace Prize and numerous other awards in recognition of her work. (Courtesy Bettmann Archives)

Mother Teresa's desire to help was intensified by the realization that leprosy, a bacterial disease that destroys skin tissue and results in terrible deformities, could be cured if caught in time. She established a number of leprosy treatment centers around the city and took treatment directly to other lepers by van. Later, Shanti Nagar, Town of Peace, was established as a community where families having one or more member afflicted with leprosy could live together in a restful, healthful setting.

Mother Teresa knew that the poorest of the poor were not confined to Calcutta. In 1959, the missionaries began to expand into other parts of India. In 1963, the Missionary Brothers of Charity were organized to work with young boys and men in places the sisters could not enter.

In 1965, Mother Teresa's Missionaries of Charity received permission from Pope John XXIII to expand their work beyond India. This was welcome news to Mother Teresa, who had seen the loneliness, sickness, and poverty of drug abusers and alcoholics in the slums of New York and London during a visit abroad in 1960. Over the next several years missions were established in places as varied as Venezuela and Tanzania, Rome and Los Angeles.

Mother Teresa's work began to attract international attention. In 1971, she was awarded the Pope John XXIII Peace Prize by the new pope, Paul VI. While her great humility made the personal attention painful, Mother Teresa understood the importance of gaining worldwide concern for the poor. Besides, the money attached to the award could certainly be put to good use.

In 1971, East Pakistan declared its independence from West Pakistan, and a bloody civil war broke out in which more than 3 million people were killed. Refugees, already the victims of unspeakable violence, suffered for lack of food, water, and shelter. Some 200,000 women, raped by soldiers, suffered the additional burdens of disgrace and pregnancy.

Mother Teresa and the Missionaries of Charity lost no time in going to the war-torn country. Where the suffering was greatest they did the most heartbreaking work. They buried the dead and arranged adoptions for unwanted babies born to women who had been raped. For this work, in 1972, Mother Teresa was given the Nehru Award by India's leader, Indira Gandhi, who said, "In an embittered world of many wars and hatred, the life and work of Mother Teresa bring new hope for the future of mankind."

Mother Teresa consistently has shown that "the Missionaries of Charity are less interested in increasing the Catholic fold than in guiding people to become the best they can be within their own religions." In 1973, she received the Templeton Prize for Progress in Religion. The panel of judges, who selected Mother Teresa's name from 2,000 nominations, included a Hindu, a Muslim, a Jew, and a Buddhist, as well as Christians.

In 1975, she presented a paper on "Women in Poverty" at the World Conference of the International Women's Year in Mexico City. While there, she visited some of Mexico's poor who lived at the edge of a huge garbage dump. Soon the Missionaries of Charity would be at work among these people.

In October 1979, it was announced that Mother Teresa had been awarded the Nobel Peace Prize. On December 9, 1979, she flew to Oslo, Norway, to receive the award. In her acceptance speech, dressed as always in a white sari and sandals, she said, "By this award the Norwegian people have recognized the existence of the poor. It is on their behalf I come." At her request, the ceremonies that year were simple. The traditional banquet was canceled, and the money that would have been spent was used to feed the poor.

Mother Teresa has been honored numerous times by her adopted country, including being awarded the Jewel of India in March 1980. In 1985, she was honored by the president of the United States, in the People's Republic of China, and in the General Assembly of the United Nations.

In recent years Mother Teresa has been hospitalized for various health problems, including heart trouble. As she ages, she finds comfort in the fact that many individuals have joined in her work. Today the Missionaries of Charity can be found in over 60 countries. Although the number of poor people in the world remains high, Mother Teresa is not discouraged, believing firmly that every individual helped counts. "It is not

> "I never experienced so perfect a sense of human equality as with Mother Teresa among her poor."
>
> —Malcolm Muggeridge

the magnitude of our actions but the amount of love that is put into them that matters," she says. The amount of love that Mother Teresa has shown the world in incalculable.

Chronology

August 27, 1910	born, Skopje, Albania (later Yugoslavia, now Serbia)
September 25, 1928	leaves home to join Sisters of Loreto
January 1929	arrives in India
1929–1946	works as a teacher and school principal in Indian convents
September 10, 1946	"Inspiration Day"—when she believes she is called to work with the poorest of the poor
August 16, 1948	leaves the convent to train and then begin her new work in Calcutta
1949	becomes a citizen of India
October 7, 1950	the Missionaries of Charity recognized as a religious order under Mother Teresa
1954	opens Nirmal Hriday, home for the dying
1955	opens Shishu Bhavan, home for orphans
1959	expands her mission within India
1965	begins international expansion of her mission
December 10, 1979	receives Nobel Peace Prize
1985	receives Medal of Honor from President Ronald Reagan
1992	hospitalized for heart trouble
1996	hospitalized for heart trouble and other illnesses

Further Reading

Clucas, Joan Graff. *Mother Teresa*. New York: Chelsea House, 1988. Biography of Mother Teresa for young people, part of the World Leaders Past and Present series. Many photographs. Includes chronology and further reading.

Gray, Charlotte. *Mother Teresa*. Milwaukee, Wisc.: Gareth Stevens, 1988. Biography of Mother Teresa for young people, part of the People Who Have Helped the World series. Many excellent photographs. Includes addresses of charitable organizations.

Spink, Kathryn. *The Miracle of Love*. San Francisco, Calif.: Harper & Row, 1981. Besides biographical information, includes excellent descriptions of the ministries of the Missionaries of Charity, founded by Mother Teresa. Contains speeches given at the ceremony where she was awarded the Nobel Peace Prize.

Peter Benenson, a British lawyer, was inspired to begin Amnesty International after reading about human rights abuses in Portugal.
(Courtesy Amnesty International)

Peter Benenson

ADVOCATE FOR JUSTICE
(1921–   )

A man on the London underground (subway) reread the article that caught his eye in the morning paper. The article said that two students in Lisbon were seen in a public cafe raising their glasses in a toast to freedom. For this they were arrested, tried, and sentenced to seven years in prison. The dictator of Portugal, António de Oliveira Salazar, forbade all unauthorized public political expressions; that included a toast to freedom.

The man who read this in his newspaper on a November morning in 1960 was an attorney named Peter Benenson. The article made him so angry that he immediately got off the train. He considered heading straight for the Portuguese embassy, but didn't think that would accomplish anything. Instead he went to a church in Trafalgar Square, sat there, and thought about how to direct his anger. He began to formulate a plan. The protest he launched would do more for freedom than the two students in Lisbon ever could have imagined.

Peter Benenson was born on July 31, 1921, to Harold and Flora Solomon. His father was a British army officer who later worked as a government official. Harold Solomon died when Peter was only nine years old. Peter's mother worked hard for many charitable causes. Flora's friends included Eleanor Roosevelt, first lady of the United States, and Chaim Weizman, the first president of Israel. Her father, Grigori Benenson, was a wealthy and respected banker-businessman in Russia who fled his country after the Communist revolution of 1917. Peter, a devout Christian, had such respect for this Jewish grandfather that he adopted the last name of Benenson.

A good student, Peter won a scholarship to Eton, a prestigious private boys' school, and continued his studies at Oxford. His studious ways did not hinder him from paying attention to what was happening in the world around him. During the Spanish Civil War (1936–1939), Peter sent money to the Spanish Relief Committee to care for an orphaned child. When Adolf Hitler rose to power in Germany, Peter and his friends raised an enormous amount of money to bring two young German Jews to England. Later, he would help find homes for other Jewish children who arrived in London as refugees

When Britain declared war on Germany in 1939, Benenson volunteered for the Royal Navy, but at first was refused because his mother was born in Russia. The next year, he was accepted and worked with an intelligence unit assigned to break German codes. After the war, he studied law and developed a strong interest in the labor movement, joining Britain's Labour Party.

In the late 1940s, the British Trade Union Congress asked Benenson to act as an official observer at several trials of trade unionists in Spain. These trials were just for show—the Spanish dictator General Francisco Franco would not allow unions to organize—and the unionists were always sent to prison. This mockery of justice made a strong impression on Benenson. Though he knew that his power as a foreign observer in these cases was limited, he made the most of it with clear disapproval of these procedures. Benenson had so many complaints about one particular trial, that during a recess he went straight to the hotel where the judge was eating his dinner to confront him personally. The next morning the defendants were set free, a direct result of Benenson's intervention. When he returned to Britain he worked with the Trade Union Congress and several members of Parliament to help the families of other imprisoned Spanish unionists.

During the 1950s, Benenson saw that some of his liberal colleagues were outraged by the racist policies of the government of South Africa, while his more conservative friends were angered by the suppression of a people's revolt in Hungary by the Communist government of the Soviet Union. To Benenson both situations were violations of human rights, and he advocated that Britain send lawyers to observe trials in both countries. Benenson went to Hungary while a colleague went to South Africa.

"First they came for the Jews and I did not speak out—because I was not a Jew. Then they came for the Communists and I did not speak out—because I was not a Communist. Then they came for the trade unionists and I did not speak out—because I was not a trade unionist. Then they came for me—and there was no one left to speak out for me."

—Attributed to Martin Niemoeller (1892–1984)

In 1959 Benenson suffered a rare affliction of the throat and stomach that required a six-month recuperation. While relaxing in Italy, he gave much thought to the necessity for dramatic and effective ways of getting people involved in the struggle for social justice. It was shortly after Benenson's return to London in November 1960 that he read of the Portuguese students' plight.

As he sat in the quiet of the church that day he decided that the time had come to involve ordinary citizens from all over the world in the human rights cause. He realized the necessity of a worldwide campaign. The release of political prisoners was what he chose for his focus.

Benenson discussed his idea with some friends, and someone suggested naming the campaign "Appeal for Amnesty, 1961." It would start on May 28, 1961, and last a year. In addition, Benenson planned to write a book he would call *Persecution 1961*, and publish an article in a leading London newspaper on launch day. He also made arrangements for a number of prominent newspapers in other countries to simultaneously carry his article.

After a great flurry of activity, launch day arrived, and Benenson was ready. In his article, he began by saying, "Open your newspaper any day of the week and you will find a report from somewhere in the world of someone being imprisoned, tortured, or executed because his opinions or religion are unacceptable to his government." He provided a few examples: Agostino Neto, an Angolan poet and doctor, beaten in front of his family and dragged away by Portuguese colonial authorities for trying to improve health care for his people; Toni Abiaticlos, a Greek Communist imprisoned in non-Communist Greece; and Josef Cardinal Mindszenty, a cleric imprisoned in Communist Hungary.

He explained his belief that "The most rapid way of bringing relief to prisoners of conscience is publicity," and that the publicity campaign he started would be "all-embracing in its composition, international in its character and politically impartial."

Benenson hoped to get peoples' attention, but the response he received was overwhelming. Letters, donations, and information on prisoners of conscience poured into Benenson's London office from around the world. Benenson was ready with a plan to capitalize on public interest. The Amnesty campaign would be comprised of groups of people who would be assigned the names of prisoners they would "adopt." These groups would then write letters to the prisoners and the prisoners' families, letting them know that someone cared. They also wrote to the people who were holding these prisoners, requesting their release. Simple, polite letters would be the nonviolent weapons of choice in this war on injustice.

The prisoners adopted would be those who had been arrested only for their ideas, people Amnesty would call "prisoners of conscience." They would be persons who had neither used nor advocated the use of violence. To guard against charges of political motivation, Benenson devised the idea of assigning Amnesty groups three prisoners each, one from an "eastern" bloc country, one from a Western country, and one from the developing world. No group would be assigned a prisoner in their own country.

The Chinese proverb, "Better to light a candle than curse the darkness," provided a powerful image to capture the spirit and meaning

"If there's lots of pressure—like from Amnesty International or some foreign countries—then we might pass them on to a judge, but if there's no pressure, then they're dead."

—Salvadoran torturer, in *The Amnesty International Handbook* of the campaign. British artist Diana Redhouse contributed the drawing of a burning candle surrounded by barbed wire that became the symbol by which Amnesty International would be known.

One of Amnesty's first adopted prisoners was Josef Beran, archbishop of Prague. Beran was imprisoned by the Nazis during World War II. Since 1949 Beran had been imprisoned by the Communist government of Czechoslovakia for delivering a sermon that protested that government's taking of power by coup. Amnesty member Sean MacBride, who served as foreign minister of Ireland, went to Prague to investigate. Amnesty groups sent countless letters and telegrams demanding the archbishop's freedom. A year and a half later, the Czech government released Beran, first to house arrest in Prague, and later to exile. Benenson and everyone involved in the Amnesty campaign was encouraged by this evidence that their methods could be successful.

The first year passed quickly as Benenson set up Amnesty groups in various places in Britain. A group was established in West Germany, followed by groups in Switzerland, Italy, and France. In 1962, a permanent international organization called Amnesty International was created. Amnesty member Sean MacBride was the first chair.

Benenson invested virtually all his money and energy in helping Amnesty grow. The intensity of his involvement began to take its toll on his health: he suffered from stomach pains and headaches. There were internal debates and controversies that added to the stress. In March 1967, Benenson withdrew from his management role with Amnesty. He had "put the ship out to sea," he said, and it was time to let others take the helm.

Amnesty continued to grow. By 1968 there were 550 groups of people writing letters on behalf of prisoners of conscience. Prisoners they had supported were freed in East Germany, Ghana, Egypt, and Burma. Some of the prisoners they supported during these and later years were famous: Václav Havel, the jailed playwright and future president of the Czech Republic, and Andrei Sakharov, the Soviet physicist, dissident, and future Nobel Peace Prize winner. Other prisoners were individuals known only to their families and close associates. One story that became well known concerned a prisoner, named Julio de Pena Valdez, a trade union leader. Valdez had been held naked in a dungeon-like cell in the Dominican Republic when Amnesty members started sending letters to his jailers. He described what happened this way:

> When the first two hundred letters came the guards gave me back my clothes. Then the next two hundred letters came and the prison director came to see me. When the next pile of letters arrived, the director got in touch with

Amnesty International continues to speak out on behalf of prisoners of conscience who might otherwise be forgotten. These Amnesty members were doing so at the United Nation's Fourth World Conference on Women in Huairou, China, in 1995. (Courtesy Bettmann Archives)

his superior. The letters kept coming and coming, three thousand of them. The President was informed. The letters kept arriving and the President called the prison to let me go. After I was released the President called me to his office for a man-to-man talk. He said: "How is it that a trade union leader like you has so many friends all over the world?" He showed me an enormous box full of letters he had received and, when we parted, he gave them to me. I still have them.

In 1974, Amnesty's chairperson, Sean MacBride, received the Nobel Peace Prize for his work on behalf of human rights. In 1977, Amnesty International itself was awarded the prize. The Amnesty representative who accepted the award accepted it in the name of "everyone who has ever written a letter asking for the release of a prisoner of conscience, everyone who has ever stood in a vigil mourning the death of a political prisoner, everyone who has ever handed out leaflets, stuffed envelopes, done the accounts. Every name on every petition counts."

A primary Amnesty focus is the use of torture by governments against their own citizens. International law outlaws torture and many of the nations of the world have signed covenants that outlaw its use. Amnesty researchers estimate that torture is used regularly by one-third of the world's governments.

> "The worldwide human–rights movement has made significant improvements in the past, and it can make more of them in the future. . . . Now the momentum must increase. It all begins with individual people caring, then doing something to help individual people in need."
>
> —John G. Healey, executive director, Amnesty International USA

Amnesty opposes the death penalty, called by the French philosopher Albert Camus "the most premeditated of murders." As of 1989, Amnesty files showed 100 nations still carrying out the death penalty.

Peter Benenson was there when Amnesty International celebrated its 20th anniversary in London in 1981. On that occasion, Benenson offered a new slogan for the organization. "I have lit this candle today," he said as he lit a large candle, "in the words of Shakespeare, 'against oblivion'—so that the forgotten prisoners should always be remembered. We work in Amnesty *against oblivion*." At the United Nation World Conference on Human Rights in Vienna, Austria, in 1993, Amnesty was a leader in bringing delegates together from 154 nations to address the issue of the abuse of human rights.

By 1994, after 33 years of effort on behalf of prisoners of conscience, Amnesty International was widely recognized as the world's largest and most respected human rights organization. Over a million members in 150 countries, over 4,000 separate local volunteer groups in 80 countries, worked to meet its goals. It is estimated that its efforts have helped liberate 25,000 political prisoners. The work of Amnesty International can be summed up in this statement made at its 25th anniversary ceremonies.

> When you do something to help a prisoner of conscience or try to save someone from torture, you are doing something of incalculable value—even if it may seem very modest to you. You are taking a stand for human dignity. . . . In the face of cruelty and the arrogant abuse of limitless power, you are proving—by personal example—to both the victims and their tormentors that compassion, justice, and human love are still alive.

Chronology

July 31, 1921	Peter Solomon born in England, later changes name to Peter Benenson after his Russian-Jewish maternal grandfather
late 1940s	acts as an observer in trials of trade unionists in Spain
1950s	continues to observe trials in other countries, including Hungary
November 1960	reads about imprisoned students in Portugal, decides to organize international campaign for justice
May 28, 1961	"Appeal for Amnesty, 1961" kicks off
1962	Amnesty International officially created
1967	Benenson withdraws from active management role
1974	Sean MacBride, Amnesty chair, wins the Nobel Peace Prize
1977	Amnesty International awarded the Nobel Peace Prize
1991	Amnesty International celebrates 30 years of human rights work

Further Reading

Amnesty International. *The Amnesty International Handbook*. Claremont Calif.: Hunter House, 1991. Details the Work of Amnesty International.

Larsen, Egon. *A Flame in Barbed Wire, The Story of Amnesty International*. New York: W.W. Norton & Co, 1979. Describes the events leading up to the founding of Amnesty International and the organization's work.

Power, Jonathan, *Amnesty International, The Human Rights Story*. New York: McGraw Hill, 1981. Describes the work of Amnesty International, the human rights organization founded by Peter Benenson.

Winner, David, *Peter Benenson, Taking a Stand Against Injustice —Amnesty International*. Milwaukee, Wisc.: Gareth Stevens, 1991. Biography for young people of the English lawyer who was motivated to stop human rights abuses, and founded Amnesty International. Part of the People Who Have Helped the World series. Includes photographs.

James Earl Carter, known as "Jimmy," was deeply concerned about human rights as president and continued to work for human rights after his term in office. (Photo by Charles Plant. Courtesy the Carter Center)

Jimmy Carter

U.S. PRESIDENT AND
WORLD CITIZEN   (1924–)

On an April morning in 1979, a group of prisoners were awakened in their small, dreary cells in the Soviet Union. They were called "dissidents" (those who disagree), and for this crime they were locked away. Now, they were told that they were no longer Soviet citizens. The prisoners were driven to an airplane and, always carefully guarded, were flown to New York City.

As the prisoners from the Soviet Union walked down a ramp from the plane, two Soviet spies that the United States had captured boarded the plane back to the Soviet Union. The newly arrived dissidents were now free for the first time in their lives, to decide where they wanted to live, with whom they wanted to associate, and to speak their minds without fear of arrest.

This remarkable exchange of prisoners had been carefully orchestrated by President Jimmy Carter, who would later call it, "a highly emotional experience for all those who were there." That night Carter would write in his diary that this activity was "one of the most significant things in a human way that we've done since I've been in office."

Jimmy Carter was born October 1, 1924, in the small town of Plains, Georgia. His father, James Earl Carter, Sr., was a successful farmer and businessman who worked quietly behind the scenes to help many of his friends and neighbors. Jimmy's mother, known to the community as Miss Lillian, was a trained nurse, and cared for anyone who needed assistance, black or white, whether or not they could pay.

After attending school in Plains, Jimmy Carter attended the U.S. Naval Academy at Annapolis, Maryland. During a visit home he began dating one of his sister's friends, Rosalynn Smith. They were married after his graduation from the Naval Academy in 1946, and Carter went to work in the U.S. nuclear submarine program. Jimmy seemed headed for a lifelong career in the navy, until his father's death in 1953. At that time he decided to quit the military to run the family's peanut business. While increasing the profitability of the peanut farming and warehousing operations, Carter served as a schoolboard member, scout master, and deacon in the Plains Baptist Church. He and Rosalynn would have four children, sons Jack, Chip, and Jeff, and daughter Amy.

In 1962, Carter became a state senator, and from 1970 to 1974 served as governor of Georgia. He then went to work for the Democratic National Committee until he announced he would run for the presidency of the United States. In his plain-spoken way he introduced himself to people around the country saying, "Hello, I'm Jimmy Carter and I'm running for president." On November 2, 1976, he narrowly defeated incumbent Gerald Ford with 51 percent of the popular vote.

The newly elected president had many ideas for social, administrative, and economic reform. But nowhere was he bolder than in calling for a U.S. foreign policy based firmly on the support of human rights. "Our commitment to human rights must be absolute," he said in his inaugural address on January 20, 1977.

This was no surprise, however. In September 1976, Carter made a campaign speech before the B'nai B'rith (an American Jewish service organization) in which he said that if elected, he would make the United States once more "a beacon of light for human rights throughout the world." In other speeches Carter said that characteristics such as honesty, integrity, fairness, liberty, justice, compassion, and love were qualities a person should have, and, he would add, "These are also the qualities that a government of human beings ought to possess." Another time, he stated, "Our country has been strongest and most effective when morality and a commitment to freedom and democracy have been most clearly emphasized in our foreign policy."

As he settled into the presidency, Carter examined the records of other nations, allies as well as enemies, on human rights. He also studied recent U.S. government actions relating to the rights of its own citizens. As a leading member of the United Nations and a signer of the Helsinki Accords and other international agreements, Carter knew that the United States could and should be held to the same standards as other nations on human rights.

At this time, support for human rights was more an idea than a policy, and it would prove to be a difficult idea to maintain in practice. Over the following months, the Carter administration would attempt to define human rights. Secretary of State Cyrus Vance described three categories of rights: "the right to be free from governmental violation of the integrity of the person" (in other words, freedom from imprisonment and torture), "the right to the fulfillment of such vital needs as food, shelter, health care, and education," and "the right to enjoy civil and political liberties" (to have a voice in government and a way to redress grievances). Another step was to put in place individuals to work for human rights. One of these was Patricia Derian, who became assistant secretary of state for human rights. She was a vocal spokesperson for the administration's goals.

On January 26, within the first week of the Carter presidency, a State Department spokesperson criticized the government of Czechoslovakia and the prime minister of Rhodesia for human rights violations. The next day the State Department took on the Soviet Union, declaring that "We have long admired Andrei Sakharov [a prominent Soviet scientist and dissident] as an outspoken champion of human rights in the Soviet Union." In response to the Soviet government's threats directed at Sakharov for his protest activities, the State Department said, "Any attempts by the Soviet authorities to intimidate Mr. Sakharov will not silence legitimate criticism in the Soviet Union and will conflict with accepted international standards in the field of human rights."

When the Soviet ambassador protested and the Soviet news agency Tass criticized the State Department, President Carter responded, saying that the statement had not been cleared with him. While he did not disagree with the statement, he seemed to indicate that he was not looking for conflict with the Soviets. "We will not comment on each and every issue," said Carter, "but we

> "The lifting of the human spirit, the revival of hope, the absence of fear, the release from prison, the end of torture, the reunion of a family, the newfound sense of human dignity—these are difficult to quantify, but I am certain that many people were able to experience them because the United States of America let it be known that we stood for freedom and justice for all people."
>
> —Jimmy Carter,
> *Keeping Faith*

As president, Carter gave a number of important speeches about human rights, including this address at Notre Dame University. (Courtesy of Jimmy Carter Library)

will from time to time comment when we see a threat to human rights, when we believe it constructive to do so."

Meanwhile, Andrei Sakharov wrote a letter to President Carter that was smuggled out of the Soviet Union. In the letter he described human rights violations committed by the Soviet government, including the persecution of a number of leading dissidents. He asked President Carter to "raise your voice" on behalf of those working for reform in the Soviet Union. Carter wrote back, saying, "You may rest assured that the American people and our government will continue our firm commitment to promote respect for human rights not only in our own country but also abroad."

Soviet dissidents were elated with the attention to their cause. Once again, the Soviet ambassador protested, and the Soviet government continued its oppression of dissidents. Soviet premier Leonid Brezhnev stated, "Washington's claims to teach others how to live, I believe, cannot be accepted by any sovereign state. . . . We will not tolerate interference in our affairs by anyone and under any pretext. A normal development of relations on such a basis is, of course, unthinkable."

The Carter administration very much wanted to complete a new treaty with the Soviet Union limiting nuclear weapons, and saw that it would have to express its human rights concerns very carefully if it wanted any cooperation from the Soviets. A speech before the United Nations General Assembly on March 17 provided Carter a good opportunity to explain that his human rights policy was not directed at any one nation. "All the signatories of the UN Charter have pledged themselves to observe and respect basic human rights," he said. "Thus no member of the United Nations can claim that mistreatment of its citizens is solely its own business." From that moment on however, Carter became more cautious about speaking out against the Soviet Union, until the second half of 1980, when the invasion of Afghanistan by the Soviets and the upcoming presidential election led him to use the strongest words since the opening weeks of his administration.

There were many other countries with dismal human rights records. In Uganda, government-sponsored violence against Christians resulted in many deaths, and, Carter said, had "disgusted the entire world." Two hundred Americans, mostly Christian missionaries and their families, were evacuated. On February 24, 1977, Secretary of State Cyrus Vance announced that aid to Argentina, Uruguay, and Ethiopia was being cut because of human rights violations. Vance also stated that the United States was concerned about human rights violations in South Korea but would not reduce military aid because of "security commitments."

During the next several years, the Carter administration was faced with a difficult dilemma when the Communist nation of Vietnam invaded its neighbor, Cambodia, ruled by one of the most vicious dictatorial regimes in the world. Over a million Cambodians died of murder or starvation as a result of the activities of Cambodian Communists, the Khmer Rouge. Certainly the Carter administration would not want to support them, but neither would they want to support the Vietnamese, who were given considerable military support by the Soviet Union. In tip-toeing through this political minefield, the Carter administration was able to do something for the refugees uprooted by the bloodshed, allowing 400,000 Southeast Asians into the United States, and giving aid for the feeding and resettlement of many more refugees in Asia.

Closer to home, Carter and his associates had to deal with the right-wing dictatorships of several Central and South American nations: El Salvador, Nicaragua, Argentina, and Chile. Politically, these countries were considered "friends," since their governments were anti–Communist. However these nations were notorious for their human rights abuses. The difficulty for the American government was that if support for these governments was withdrawn over the human rights issue, they might very well be toppled by pro–Communist forces, which might create an even worse environment for human rights.

"War is the greatest violation of basic human rights that one people can inflict upon another. Starvation, exposure, and disease caused by war often produce more casualties than the fighting itself."

—Jimmy Carter, *Talking Peace*

In late 1979 and through 1980, the Carter administration had many major problems to resolve, including the taking of American hostages at the U.S. embassy in Iran, the Soviet invasion of Afghanistan, the domestic fuel and economic crises, and a re-election campaign. In the campaign, Republican challenger Ronald Reagan criticized the Carter administration's human rights policy. When the American people voted in November 1980, Reagan won.

On January 14, 1981, shortly before the new president would be inaugurated, Carter gave a speech in which he said, "For a few minutes now, I want to lay aside my role as leader of one nation, and speak to you as a fellow citizen of the world about three issues—the threat of nuclear destruction, our stewardship of the physical resources of the planet, and the preeminence of the basic rights of human beings." He spoke movingly of "the essential unity of our species and our planet."

Had the Carter human rights initiative been successful? There are a number of ways to look at that question. Carter *had* succeeded in getting human rights issues publicized. After his first year in office, the International League for Human Rights said,

> Within the past year, human rights has for the first time become a subject of national policy debate in many countries. Human rights concerns have been the focus of discussion in international organizations and of greater attention in the world media. A most significant factor in this has been President Carter and the U.S. human rights policy.

Historian Arthur Schlesinger said that the Carter policy "had placed human rights on the world's agenda—and on the world's conscience."

Though talk was not necessarily always translated into action, and sometimes got him into trouble with the nations he criticized, Carter would write in his memoirs, "I was often criticized, here and abroad, for aggravating other government leaders and straining international relations. At the same time, I was never criticized by the people who were imprisoned or tortured or otherwise deprived of basic rights."

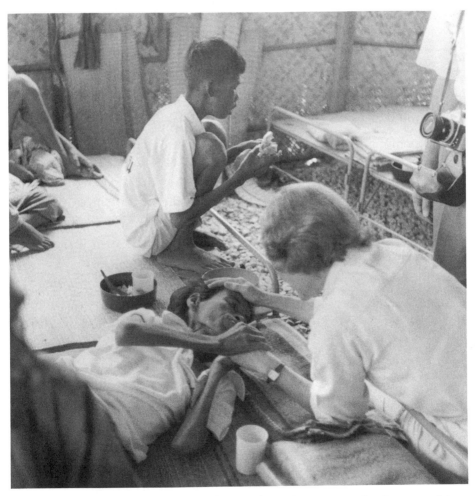

Putting words into action. First Lady Rosalynn Carter visited refugees at this camp in Southeast Asia. (Courtesy Jimmy Carter Library)

After the inauguration of Ronald Reagan, Carter returned to Georgia with Rosalynn. He completed his memoirs, and in 1982 he opened the Carter Center, an organization that works on behalf of humanity. "At the center I planned to address the issues of education, health, the environment, human rights, and of course, global conflict," he wrote in *Talking Peace.* "Most of all I wanted the Carter Center to be a place where people from all walks of life and all religious and ethnic backgrounds could come to seek peaceful resolutions to troubling and complicated problems." The work of Jimmy Carter on behalf of human rights had only just begun.

In 1989, Carter traveled to Panama as an international observer to monitor elections. The next year he did the same in Nicaragua. In 1994 he traveled to Haiti to speak with leaders of the junta who refused to yield power to the democratically elected government. Even as American troops prepared to invade Haiti, Carter continued to negotiate. At literally the last possible moment, the junta leaders signed an agreement, and the invasion was called off, averting a potentially bloody conflict. Again and again, Carter would visit the world's most troubled places, seeking peace and justice for all people. Carter Center programs support efforts to increase grain production in famine-striken countries and programs to eliminate such health scourges as Guinea worm disease and river blindness. One week of every

> "Those close to Jimmy Carter understand what makes him one of the unique American leaders of the twentieth century. We know his compassion, his intelligence, his determination, his uncompromising honesty and his bedrock faith."
>
> —Actor Kirk Douglas at Carter's 70th birthday party in 1994

year he and Rosalynn help build homes for needy people with an organization called Habitat for Humanity; he calls it one of the best weeks of every year. To help fight deprivation in the United States, he helped start the Atlanta Project, through which he meets some of America's most needy citizens and helps them improve their lives.

Former President Carter has received numerous awards and acknowledgments for his work to benefit humanity. In 1984, he received the World Methodist Peace Award. In 1987, he was the recipient of the Albert Schweitzer Prize for Humanitarianism, and in 1990 he was given the Liberty Medal. In 1992, the President of Guyana awarded Carter the Order of Excellence, that nation's highest honor, for his involvement in the restoration of democracy to that country. Carter is also involved in awarding annually a prestigious human rights award, the Carter-Menil Human Rights Prize, to people he calls "human rights heroes."

Jimmy Carter knows that the struggle for human rights is not over. "The abuse of human rights is still a serious problem in too many lands," he wrote in 1982, and it remains true today. All the more reason to keep faith, and keep trying.

Chronology

October 1, 1924	Jimmy Carter born, Plains, Georgia
1953	leaves the Navy to run the family peanut farming and warehousing business
1962	elected state senator
1970	elected governor of Georgia
November 1976	elected president of the United States

January 1977	inaugurated, immediately declares human rights a high priority, corresponds with Soviet dissident Andrei Sakharov
1977–1980	Carter administration deals with human rights crises around the world, including Argentina, Uganda, and Cambodia
November 1980	defeated in re-election bid by Ronald Reagan
1982	founds the Carter Center as a place to work toward peace and human rights goals
1986	cofounds the Carter-Menil Foundation to promote protection of human rights
1989	monitors elections in Panama
1994	helps negotiate peace agreement in Haiti, travels to former Yugoslavia to support peace efforts there
1995	pursues goal of eradicating Guinea worm disease through Carter Center efforts

Further Reading

Carter, Jimmy. *Talking Peace*. New York: Dutton Children's Books, 1993. Written for young people, explaining his vision for world peace, democracy, and human rights. Details the purpose of the Carter Center and Carter's post–presidency work.

Dumbull, John. *The Carter Presidency, A Re-evaluation*. Manchester, England: Manchester University Press, 1993. Looks at both the strengths and weaknesses of the Carter years.

Muravchik, Joshua. *The Uncertain Crusade, Jimmy Carter and the Dilemmas of Human Rights Policy*. Lanham Md.: Hamilton Press, 1986. This book examines in detail the problems the Carter administration faced in attempting to give human rights issues a high priority.

Smith, Betsy Covington. *Jimmy Carter, President.* New York: Walker and Co., 1986. Biography for young people, follows the life and career of Carter through the presidency.

Desmond Tutu, archbishop of South Africa, labored long and hard to help bring down the system of apartheid in that country. Here, he speaks to members of the United Nations Correspondents Association. (UN Photo 164 865/Milton Grant)

MINISTERING TO
SOUTH AFRICA   (1931–)

The police estimated that over 3,000 people filed into the sports stadium in Duduza Township on that chilly day in July, 1985. July is a winter month in South Africa, and these people did not come joyfully to watch a sporting event. They came in sorrow, and in anger. The occasion was a funeral, yet another funeral, for people killed in the protest against the government's racial policies.

The Anglican bishop of Johannesburg stood to address the crowd, a sea of faces. The bishop was older than many of the people in the crowd, especially the young men carrying the coffin, but his face, too, was black. He was Desmond Tutu, the first black bishop of Johannesburg, and he tried to find words to acknowledge the sorrow and channel the anger of the mourners.

A short while later, as people left the stadium, Tutu saw that members of the crowd were attacking a man they believed was a police spy. The man's car had already been set on fire, and now the crowd seemed intent on doing the same to him.

Tutu knew that the police often treated the black people of South Africa with brutality. He was an outspoken critic of the government and its racial policies. He also believed that the worst thing that black South Africans could do was to debase themselves by employing the same cruel tactics.

> Without thought for his own safety, Bishop Tutu
> pushed his way into the crowd and allowed the beaten
> man to escape. Tutu could only wonder how many more
> lives would be lost in this struggle, how many more
> funerals there would be.

Zachariah and Aletta Tutu had a daughter and two sons who died in infancy, before a son, Desmond, was born on October 7, 1931. He was a sickly baby and very nearly died. When he recovered, he was given the name Mpilo, which means life.

It was Desmond Mpilo Tutu's fate to be born in the Republic of South Africa. Despite the fact that descendants of European colonists made up less than 20 percent of the population, they controlled the government. Desmond's parents, descendants of the Xhosas and Tswanas, and other native tribes, were not allowed to vote or to exercise many other rights, despite the fact that blacks were a majority of the population.

Growing up in Klerksdorp, Desmond learned the realities of life for a black person in South Africa. He saw that white children received free schooling and free lunches, though their parents had ample resources to provide these themselves. The few black children who were able to go to mission schools were charged a fee and received no free lunch, though there was little money for food in *their* homes. White children lived in town, while the black children lived in neighborhoods set aside for them outside of town called "locations."

In 1943, when Desmond was 12, his family moved to Sophiatown, a neighborhood in Johannesburg where blacks, Coloureds (people of mixed races), and Asians were allowed to buy land and homes. There Desmond attended Western Native Township High School, popularly known as Madibane, after its principal.

Desmond did well in high school, and hoped to go on to medical school. He was frail and knew firsthand about sickness, especially after contracting tuberculosis at the age of 14. An Anglican priest, Father Trevor Huddleston, visited him often during the long months while he recovered, bringing him both books and encouragement. Father Huddleston was a kindly man, one of the few whites Desmond encountered who treated black South Africans with respect.

Though Desmond scored high on his exams for admission to medical school, his family could not afford the fees. Disappointed, he had to settle for a segregated teacher's college, Pretoria Bantu Normal College. "Bantu," was what the government called black South Africans. Under laws passed in 1948, the year Desmond graduated from high school, black South Africans were further oppressed. In that year the Afrikaners, descendants of European colonists, won a majority in Parliament, and their Nationalist Party created oppressive new laws and restrictions. One of the most hated was the pass law, which required that black South Africans over 18 years of age carry a pass at all times with their name and photo on it. If they were caught anywhere without the pass, they could be arrested.

All these laws, which were designed to keep the races strictly segregated, were known as apartheid—"apartness." As the laws went into effect, black South Africans did what they could to protest, but there was little they could do without facing arrest or worse. In 1952, a Defiance Campaign was initiated by an opposition group called the African National Congress (ANC), led by Oliver Tambo and Nelson Mandela. Some 8,000 protesters were arrested and the laws remained in force.

Meanwhile, Desmond Tutu was completing teacher's training. In 1954, he returned to Madibane as a teacher. On July 2, 1955, he married fellow teacher Leah Nomalizo Shenxane.

Desmond Tutu aspired to be a good teacher, but the Nationalist government made that all but impossible. Government policy said that blacks should be educated only as befitted their Bantu status. Blacks were to be taught only in their tribal languages, which would make it difficult for them to function in the white, English-speaking society. Important subjects such as math were not considered appropriate.

In 1957, despite being parents of a one-year-old named Trevor, Desmond and Leah Tutu both resigned rather than submit to teaching under the Bantu education program. Desmond now turned to preaching—one of the few options left to him—a career he saw as "a likely means of service." With the support of his old friend Father Huddleston, Tutu went through two years of training at St. Peter's Theological College and was ordained a priest of the Anglican church in 1961. By this time he and Leah were parents of three children (son Trevor, and two daughters, Thandeka and Naomi).

The protests against apartheid continued. Nelson Mandela was tried for treason for his part in the protests. After being acquitted, Mandela worked for the ANC "underground." On March 21, 1960, Robert Sobukwe, leader of a group called the Pan-African Congress, organized a protest against the pass laws. That day, police opened fire on a crowd that gathered outside a police station at the black township of Sharpeville. Reports said that the police kept shooting as people in the crowd tried to flee. When it was over, 67 people had been killed and 186 were wounded.

> "I believe history teaches us that once a people are determined to become free, then nothing can stop them from reaching their goal."
>
> —Desmond Tutu in
> *The Words of Desmond Tutu*

People around the world were shocked when they heard about the "Sharpeville Massacre." The South African government responded by declaring a state of emergency, and gave the police greater powers to arrest and detain anyone in the name of keeping order. The African National Congress and the Pan–African Congress were declared illegal. Sobukwe was arrested and imprisoned for nine years and then banned from speaking in public. Oliver Tambo went into exile outside the country and Nelson Mandela went into hiding.

While black South Africans were forced to endure oppression in their homeland, in 1962 Tutu earned the opportunity to travel to England and study at King's College, Cambridge University, by scoring higher on a special exam than all other Anglican priests in South Africa. Desmond and his family found the freedom of England liberating. "We didn't have to carry our passes anymore," he remembered, "and we did not have to look around to see if we could use that bath or that exit."

The Tutu's fourth child (a daughter, Mpho) was born in England, but after four years, it was time to return to their own country. There, they found that things were not any better for black South Africans than when they'd left. In 1963, Nelson Mandela was sentenced to life in prison. The Tutus again had to submit to discrimination. Desmond was able to get a job at a seminary. He taught black theology—the view that Christianity could help blacks end apartheid, that Christianity could help people be free, even the black people of South Africa.

In 1972, Tutu was asked to work with the World Council of Churches in Britain. The South African government hesitated to issue him a passport: the World Council of Churches supported the African National Congress and the Pan–African Congress in their efforts to end apartheid. Tutu was determined that he would not be denied this opportunity. He appealed directly to Prime Minister John Vorster, and he eventually received his passport.

Tutu's job was to train ministers, especially black ministers in Africa. For the next three years, while he and his family lived in London, he traveled often to Africa and Asia. He began to gain confidence in speaking to people of all nations and races. Tutu saw the results of violent confrontations in many places, including Uganda, Vietnam, and Northern Ireland, and was convinced that there had to be a better way for people to solve problems other than through violence.

Tutu returned to South Africa when named dean of Johannesburg in 1975, the first time a black man was given that title. Special permission was granted for the Tutus to live in the dean's house in Johannesburg—permission Tutu didn't want to accept—so the Tutu family lived in Soweto, the huge South West Township for blacks outside of Johannesburg. A million and a half people lived there in 100,000 government-built cement homes and countless shacks made from scraps of metal and wood. Soweto was an abominable place, full of anger and frustration, especially among the young people. Tutu understood the injustice that fed that anger but urged a nonviolent response. He feared that it was only a matter of time before there would be trouble, and he was right. On June 16, 1976, 15,000 schoolchildren marched

"Africans believe in something that is difficult to render in English. We call it *obuntu, botho*. It means the essence of being human. . . . It speaks about humaneness, gentleness, hospitality, putting yourself out on behalf of others, being vulnerable. . . . It recognizes that my humanity is bound up in yours, for we can only be human together."

—Desmond Tutu in *The Words of Desmond Tutu*

Under apartheid, millions of South African blacks were forced to settle in so-called homelands where they lived in terrible conditions—it was the largest forced movement of people in peacetime history. Pictured here is Ezakheni, a village in the Kwa Zulu "homeland" in Natal, South Africa. (United Nations Photo 151 707)

through the streets of Soweto, many shouting "Down with Afrikaans"—(the language of the European colonists, which they were supposed to be taught). Once again, police suddenly opened fire, and a thirteen-year-old boy was shot dead. In the rioting that broke out, hundreds more were killed.

In the police crackdown that followed, Winnie Mandela, wife of the imprisoned ANC leader, and Steve Biko, a black journalist, were arrested. Their actions inspired pride in black Africans. In 1977, Steve Biko was beaten to death while in police custody.

In February 1978, Tutu was named general secretary of the South African Council of Churches (SACC), a part of the World Council of Churches. Already controversial for its support of the anti–apartheid movement, under Tutu's leadership SACC became even more involved in the struggle for social justice.

Tutu discouraged foreign countries from investing in South Africa, and asked them to boycott South African goods, such as gold and coal, as a protest against apartheid. The Polaroid Company stopped selling the government of South Africa the material it used in the making of the hated passes. Tutu believed that this economic pressure was a powerful weapon of nonviolence, despite the fact that the black population as well as the government would be hurt by the economic pressure. "It is no use being well-to-do when you are a slave," Tutu said.

In the fall of 1984, while teaching for a semester in New York City, Tutu learned that he had been awarded the Nobel Peace Prize. He said that the news meant that "Justice is going to win." The government of South Africa, of course, was not so pleased. The Nationalist press called him "a troublemaker." At the awards ceremony, the Prize Committee chairman said "On a broad front a campaign is being fought . . . for truth, freedom and justice. In recognition of the fact that it is this alternative which must succeed, the South African bishop, Desmond Tutu, has been selected as this year's Peace Prize laureate." The $192,000 awarded with the medal was used to fund a scholarship for African youths.

In 1985, Tutu was named Anglican bishop of Johannesburg, but there was little else to celebrate in South Africa that year, a year of violent confrontations between the police and protesters, and even between various groups of protesters. Between July 1985 and March 1986, some 8,000 people were detained by security forces in various incidents.

In September 1986, Tutu became archbishop of Cape Town, head of the Anglican church in South Africa. That year he was awarded the Carter-Menil Human Rights Prize and the Martin Luther King Jr. Peace Award. Yet, as he reminded his friends around the world, he was not eligible to vote in the land of his birth, simply because of the color of his skin. When criticized for being too political, he said it would be easier for him to be less political if all the black political leaders weren't put in jail—as Mandela was—exiled—in Tambo's case—or killed—as were so many, including Steve Biko.

During the following years, the Nationalist Party continued to maintain apartheid, even in the face of increasing international pressure. In February 1990, Nelson Mandela was finally released from prison. The government, headed by F.W. de Klerk, declared it would work with black leaders to create a new political system that would allow *all* South Africans to participate. The next year, many of the apartheid laws were repealed, but violence among the various factions within South Africa increased drastically and threatened to kill the hopes for a peaceful change in the government. "By fighting and engaging in violent acts we give others the excuse to say we are not ready to govern ourselves," Tutu angrily warned the people.

In April 1994, the day 63-year-old Desmond Tutu had waited and worked for all his adult life arrived when for the first time he was finally able to vote in an election open equally to members of all races. The election resulted in Nelson Mandela's presidency. As Tutu said, "It is a victory for all South Africans. It is a victory for democracy and freedom." On May 9, 1994, at a celebration honoring the new government, Tutu said, "We of many cultures, languages and races are become one nation. We are the Rainbow People of God."

Looking back, Tutu says apartheid failed both because it was evil

"You cannot hold people down forever, because people are made for something more glorious."

—Desmond Tutu in *The Rainbow People of God*

and made neither political nor economic sense. Looking forward, he sees many problems yet to be overcome, largely as a result of the years of apartheid. It was easy to know who the enemy was then, he says. "Now it won't be so easy to say what me must march for." There are many different opinions about what it will take to improve human rights in South Africa and how to go about it. Questions of land rights, jobs for the unemployed, education for those for whom schooling has long been neglected, and what to do about past abuses under apartheid will be difficult to settle. It is certain that the voice of Desmond Tutu will be one of those raised to define the future of the disadvantaged people of South Africa.

Chronology

1931	Desmond Tutu is born in Klerksdorp, South Africa
1948	Nationalist Party government passes apartheid laws
1954	Tutu begins career as teacher
1955	marries Leah Shenxane
1957	leaves teaching, prepares for Anglican priesthood
March 21, 1960	Sharpeville Massacre
1975	becomes dean of Johannesburg
June 16, 1976	Soweto riots
1978	becomes Secretary General of South African Council of Churches
December 10, 1984	awarded Nobel Peace Prize
1985	becomes bishop of Johannesburg
1986	named Archbishop of Cape Town, head of Anglican church in South Africa

February 10, 1990	Nelson Mandela released
April 1994	votes in first national election open to members of all races in South Africa and Nelson Mandela becomes president of South Africa
April 1996	Truth and Reconciliation Commission, headed by Tutu begins investigating abuses committed during apartheid
July 1996	becomes archbishop emeritus

Further Reading

Bentley, Judith. *Archbishop Tutu of South Africa*. Hillside, N.J.: Enslow Publishers, 1988. Biography of Tutu for young people. Published before the transition of power in South Africa. Includes the Nobel Peace Prize acceptance speech.

DuBoulay, Shirley. *Tutu, Voice of the Voiceless*. Grand Rapids Mich.: William Eerdman's Publishing Co., 1988. In–depth biography of Tutu from his childhood to becoming Archbishop of Cape Town.

Tutu, Desmond, and John Allen, ed. *The Rainbow People of God*. New York: Doubleday, 1994. Through the use of Tutu's sermons and speeches, provides insight into Tutu's feelings and attitudes during the fight to end apartheid, through the elections of 1994. Includes the Nobel lecture.

Tutu, Naomi and Desmond Tutu. *The Words of Desmond Tutu*. New York: Newmarket Press, 1989. Small book of prayers, speeches, and quotations from Tutu, with an introduction by his daughter.

Hebe de Bonafini, leader of the Mothers of the Plaza, has refused to be silenced about the Argentines who disappeared during what became known as the "Dirty War." (Courtesy Asociación Madres de Plaza de Mayo)

Hebe de Bonafini
and
María Adela de Antokoletz

MOTHERS OF THE PLAZA DE MAYO

It's a Thursday afternoon and for Hebe de Bonafini that means she will go to the square known as the Plaza de Mayo in Buenos Aires, Argentina's capital. There she will walk around and around a stone monument. She will be joined by other women. It is not merely her feet that she will be exercising as she paces the square. It will be her rights as a mother, as a citizen of Argentina, and as a human being—her right to know what happened to her children when they disappeared long ago. It was then that she became one of the Mothers of the Plaza de Mayo.

Argentina is a country with a turbulent history. Spaniards came in the 16th century and made war on and spread disease among the native people. One group or another has been struggling for power ever since. In 1946, Juan Perón, a military leader, became president by promising to improve conditions for the nation's workers, most of whom were very poor. These workers adored Perón and his wife Evita, but others hated him for his curtailment of their rights, including freedom of press and speech. In 1955, Perón was forced to flee to Spain when the military took over Argentina, but he returned and was re-elected president in 1973. When Perón died the next year, his third wife, Isabel Perón, briefly succeeded him. During this time there was a great deal of violence in the streets of Argentina, mostly between left-wing groups—the Montoneros, and right–wing groups—the Triple A.

On March 24, 1976, military leaders again seized control of the government, claiming this was the only way to restore order to Argentina. Many Argentines agreed and hoped that the junta, or military government, could stop the violence and restore the failing economy. Argentines knew the military would crack down on the Montoneros and other anti-government guerrillas, but that involved only a relatively small number of people, and it seemed a small price to pay for safety in the streets.

Even when Argentines started hearing rumors that large numbers of people were being arrested and that many others were mysteriously disappearing, it was easy to convince themselves that the government had a good reason for what it was doing: those arrested had to be guilty of something. Nothing was being reported in the carefully monitored newspapers and TV shows that would make the government look bad.

Slowly, however, a growing number of people began to realize that something very wrong was happening in Argentina. It was as if the government was fighting a war, an undeclared war, against its own people. The military leaders called it the Process of National Reorganization. Some of them even called it World War III—they were determined to wipe out all "subversives" in Argentina once and for all. Their definition of subversive was expanded to include not only those who committed an act of violence but those who knew someone who had committed an act of violence, or even someone who might think of sympathizing with the philosophy of the offenders. The activities of the government between 1976 and 1983 became known as the "Dirty War."

María Adela de Antokoletz worked in the law courts in Buenos Aires, where she could often see her son, Daniel Víctor, who practiced law. María was very close to her son, and worried about his representation of political prisoners in court. He'd already been beaten as a warning, and she feared that something worse would happen. Daniel thought his reputation as a defender of human rights and his connections with the Organization of American States and the United Nations would protect him. He was wrong. On November 10, 1976, he was arrested, handcuffed, hooded, and taken away. His wife was also arrested. She was released after a week, but before being released, a guard let her see her husband for a few minutes. It was clear he had been badly tortured. Neither she nor his mother heard anything more about Daniel Víctor.

Mrs. Antokoletz tried to find out what had happened to her son. Eventually she went to the Ministry of the Interior, where a small office had been set up for people who wanted to report a "disappearance." Officials made fun of the women who came there, telling them their sons had run off with other women. It was obvious they had no intention of helping; they wouldn't admit that the government had taken their children.

Finally, one of the women in the minister's office said furiously, "It's not here that we ought to be—it's the Plaza de Mayo. And when there's enough of us, we'll go to the Casa Rosada and see the President about our children who are missing." Her name was Mrs. Azucena de De Vicenti. Later she, too, would "disappear." She is presumed to have been murdered by the government.

On that day in the minister's office, something began. On Saturday, April 13, 1977, 14 women, including Mrs. Antokoletz, met at the Plaza de Mayo. The plaza was a public square surrounded by business and government offices. At one end was the Casa Rosada where the president's offices were located. The women knew that it was dangerous to protest in this place; it might cost them their lives. However, these were mothers whose children had been abducted, and they were willing to put their lives on the line to find out what had happened. The mothers carried only their identity cards, and a few coins for the bus ride home. They wore flat shoes in case they had to run from the police. Arriving one by one, they walked around the center of the plaza. It was a Saturday afternoon however, and there were few people around to notice them. They decided to come back on the following Friday when they could make a more significant protest.

A few months earlier, on February 8, 1977, Jorge Omar Bonafini a 33-year-old man, returned home from the university where he worked as a physicist to find his house ransacked and a group of men waiting for him. The neighbors saw him being put into the trunk of a car, the kind of car the security police were known to drive. It looked like he was unconscious. When his mother, Hebe de Bonafini, came to his house to see what had happened, she found blood on the floor of the bathroom.

In 1978, Jorge's estranged wife was taken from a friend's house by the police. A short time later, 31-year-old Raúl Alfredo Bonafini, Mrs. de Bonafini's other son, was taken, too. All of them disappeared without a trace and were never heard from or seen again. None of them had ever been involved in violence. The "worst" they had ever done was to be involved with trade unions.

When Jorge disappeared, Mrs. de Bonafini was told that she should get a writ of habeas corpus, a paper stating that a detained person must be brought before a court or judge. It literally means that you should "have the body." The government would not admit to having arrested Jorge. In their book *The Disappeared and the Mothers of the Plaza*, authors Simpson and Bennett, describe how she went from police stations to army centers and prisons, and found that "she was seeing the same faces as she waited forlornly on the hard wooden benches in small, inhospitable offices or in echoing corridors: the faces of other mothers who had also lost their children and could get no news of where they were."

One of these women told her of a group of women who were planning to meet at the Plaza de Mayo to protest the disappearances; Mrs. de Bonafini decided to join them. It was Friday, April 19, 1977, the second meeting of the Mothers of the Plaza de Mayo. At 5:00 that evening, the women began to walk around the monument. They gathered again the next Friday, and the next. A few more women came each time, and the police began to take notice. They asked the women to show their identification cards and wrote down their names. The police forced the women to leave, but the women were determined to return. The mothers even switched their protest from Friday to Thursday, when the Plaza would be even busier and their protest would get more notice.

As their numbers grew, the harassment increased. At first the police merely threatened the women, but then they began to make arrests. Still the women came. Now, besides mothers, there were grandmothers, wives, sisters, and daughters, too. As Simpson and Bennett wrote, "It ceased to be a movement which was simply concerned with the fate of their own immediate relatives, and became a protest on behalf of everyone who had disappeared."

People began to talk about these "Mothers of the Plaza." Sometimes they were called "Las Locas de la Plaza," the Mad Women of the Plaza. That didn't bother them. As Mrs. de Antokoletz told authors Simpson and Bennett, "We must have been crazy to challenge the government at that time. But our craziness came from our feelings of pain and grief."

Word of what the mothers were doing spread through Buenos Aires despite the fact that none of the Spanish-language newspapers dared report these activities. The Mothers raised money among themselves, and on October 5, 1977, they ran a paid advertisement listing the names of those who had disappeared. It was risky for the newspapers to accept this advertisement, and they charged a high rate. The Mothers wrote: "We do not ask for anything more than the truth."

On Thursday afternoons the Mothers gathered, silently protesting the disappearances, despite inclement weather and the very real threat to their own safety. (Courtesy Asociación Madres de Plaza de Mayo)

Pictures of some of the missing were included, signed with their mother's names.

The advertisement had the effect the Mothers wanted; their protest was getting harder for people to ignore. A week and a half after the advertisement appeared, several hundred women took a petition bearing 24,000 signatures to the congress building, demanding an investigation into the disappearances. Foreign journalists interviewed some of the Mothers; Argentine newspeople dared not do so. The government's response was to increase the harassment of the Mothers.

On Thursday, December 8, 1977, the Mothers met at a church in Buenos Aires, planning another advertisement. As they left the meeting, a group of armed men was waiting. A number of Mothers and a French nun were arrested and taken away. All the money the Mothers raised for their advertisement was taken. Two days later the mother who had started the movement, Azucena de De Vicenti, and other protesters, were arrested. None of them were ever seen again.

This devastated the Mothers, both as individuals and as a group. They wanted to believe that even the brutal Argentine government could not be so cruel as to do violence to a group of mothers (and foreign nuns) concerned only about their missing loved ones. Now they knew that they were wrong.

On the Thursday after the arrests, instead of the usual 200 or 300 women, only about 40 marched in the Plaza de Mayo. Those that came were determined to continue the protest, despite that on any given week, some of them might be arrested. The government tried to blame the disappearances on other groups, but the Mothers called a press conference with foreign journalists to stand by the truth that it was the government that was kidnapping their loved ones.

At times the police would have the Plaza de Mayo blocked off to such an extent that the Mothers could only dash in for a few moments before being hauled away; sometimes they were forced to meet somewhere else. A few priests allowed them to meet in their churches, but it was illegal, so they would only sit silently in the dark, praying and passing around notes with whatever information was available.

Slowly the military junta began to feel the wrath of the international community. The U.S. Congress and President Jimmy Carter sharply criticized the Argentine government. First Lady Rosalynn Carter wrote to the Mothers of the Plaza, expressing her support. When one of Argen-

"It was the willingness of the Mothers to take action that kept the flame of opposition burning in public view during the worst years; only they had the necessary madness to do it."

—Simpson and Bennett
in *The Disappeared
and the Mothers of the Plaza*

tina's government leaders went to Italy, he came back and reported, "They hate us there." Gradually the number of arrests began to decline.

In September 1979, the Organization of American States' Inter-American Commission on Human Rights visited Argentina. Six men interviewed many people during a period of two weeks. As Simpson and Bennett wrote:

> The report which the commission produced was the most effective counter to the argument that the repression in Argentina had been exaggerated; in 266 concisely written and unemotional pages, it listed dozens of cases and called on the Argentine Government to bring to trial those responsible for the deaths of those who had disappeared, and to make significant changes in the way in which the emergency powers were being used. . . . The military authorities ignored the recommendations, but were not able to ignore the report itself . . . it was no longer possible for the Argentine authorities to pretend that gross violations of human rights had not occurred.

By 1980, the Mothers had taken steps to become an official organization—electing officers, opening a bank account, and setting up an office. They decided that they would go back to meeting and marching in the Plaza de Mayo, and continue until either they got their answers or were killed.

On Thursday, January 3, 1980, at about 3:30 in the afternoon, the Mothers went to the plaza. The few police that were there seemed surprised to see them; apparently they thought the organization had been destroyed. The next week the square was filled with policemen, but the Mothers were determined, and despite threats and beatings and from time to time a few arrests, the Mothers continued to come each Thursday, wearing their flat shoes and white scarves with their children's names on them. Thursday after Thursday, month after month, year after year, they marched, demanding information about their children. According to Argentine human rights organizations, estimates of the number of disappeared ranged between 8,000 and 30,000.

In December 1980, the Nobel Peace Prize was given to Adolfo Pérez Esquivel, an architect and advocate of nonviolence who condemned the murders of military leaders by left-wing Montoneros before the junta took over, and later decried the repression of the military government against leftists and others. He was involved with international human rights organizations and supported the Mothers of the Plaza. Esquivel was imprisoned by the military for over a year and the Nobel Peace Prize was a boost for those fighting the repression in Argentina.

Perhaps as a last-ditch effort to get the country united behind them, the junta launched an attack on a group of islands off the coast of Argentina. The Argentines called them the Islas Malvinas, and claimed possession. The British government called them the Falklands. The islands were home to about 2,000 people, mostly sheepherders with English citizenship. The British government responded more strongly to the attack than the Argentines expected. After a little more than two months and 2,000 lives lost, the Falklands/Malvinas War ended in June 1982, with the Argentines defeated and the military humiliated. The already precarious economy was devastated, and the military lost its ability to command power.

Free elections were finally held in October 1983. Raúl Alfonsín, a critic of the military government who promised to investigate the disappearances, was elected. He was inaugurated on December 10, 1983. Nobel Prize win-

"[The importance of the movement was] above all, raising people's awareness so that what happened here will never happen again. Here or anywhere."

—Mrs. Antokoletz, quoted in *The Disappeared and the Mothers of the Plaza*

Long after the junta was toppled, the Mothers continued to gather to call for justice. Hebe de Bonafini is pictured here, speaking to a crowd in 1992.
(Courtesy Asociación Madres de Plaza de Mayo)

ner Adolfo Pérez Esquivel was at the inauguration. So were Hebe de Bonafini and María Adela de Antokoletz, who had become president and vice president, respectively, of the Mothers of the Plaza de Mayo. Outside the Casa Rosada, in the Plaza de Mayo itself, women were gathered. Mostly, they were cheering, though some were crying for those who did not live to see this day, those who never would be seen again. The Mothers hoped and prayed that this signalled the end of repression in Argentina, and the perpetrators of the Dirty War would be punished. Having helped bring down the terrorist government in Argentina, they were now looking beyond their own borders. Some of them chanted "Argentina today, Chile and Uruguay tomorrow."

Alfonsín set up a commission to investigate the disappearances. The commission, known as CONADEP, established that nearly 9,000 of the disappeared could be identified by name;

almost all of them were presumed dead. The vast majority were between the ages of 20 and 35, though some were very old and some very young. An additional 20,000 people had been officially arrested during the Dirty War, many of whom were tortured before being released. Two million Argentines fled the country to avoid such persecution.

The military stalled and delayed, but eventually the junta leaders were brought to trial and, in December 1985, a few of them were convicted and received prison sentences. None of them had to undergo anything like the cruel treatment of those who had been imprisoned during the Dirty War. With time, even the few who had been sentenced were pardoned and released from jail.

The Mothers of the Plaza de Mayo continued to march for truth and justice. The government was seeking "reconciliation" and stability. A "full stop" to any further trials of persons involved in the Dirty War was ordered.

Another election was held on May 14, 1989, and a Perónist named Carlos Saúl Menem was elected president. In 1990 Menem issued a pardon to all those convicted of crimes committed during the Dirty War, in an effort to put the matter to rest. There were others, such as former navy officer Adolfo Scilingo, who believed there was more to be said. He came forward in 1995 with a confession to having participated in the dumping of prisoners, drugged but alive, from planes flying over the Atlantic Ocean during the Dirty War.

"They were unconscious. We stripped them, and when the flight commander gave the order, we opened the door and threw them out, naked, one by one. That is the story, and nobody can deny it."

—Argentine Navy Captain Adolfo Scilingo, quoted in *Time* magazine, March 27, 1995

As to the Mothers of the Plaza de Mayo, they have split into two groups with different approaches to the human rights problems in Argentina. Hebe de Bonafini is the leader of one, and María Adela de Antokoletz is leader of the other. They still march together on Thursday afternoons, and continue to hold an annual "Day of Remembering" each year. For them it is impossible to forget.

Chronology

1973	Isabel Perón succeeds her husband as president of Argentina; internal violence escalates during following years
March 24, 1976	military junta seizes control
1976–1980	the worst years of the Dirty War against the people of Argentina
April 13, 1977	the first group of Mothers march in the Plaza de Mayo, demanding information about their "disappeared" children
October 5, 1977	Mothers of the Plaza de Mayo run an advertisement in the newspapers, raising awareness about the disappearances
December 8, 1977	a nun and several of the Mothers are arrested and "disappear" after a meeting
September 1979	Organization of the American States sends a commission to Argentina, reports on the disappearances
1980	Mothers of the Plaza de Mayo becomes an official organization
December 1980	Adolfo Pérez Esquivel, human rights supporter, wins the Nobel Peace Prize
June 1982	Argentina is defeated in the Falklands/Malvinas War; junta begins to lose control

October 1983	Raúl Alfonsín is elected in a democratic election, promises to investigate disappearances
December 10, 1983	the democratically elected government takes office
September 21, 1984	CONADEP report published, documenting the disappearances
1987	Mothers split into two groups, Asociación Madres de Plaza de Mayo, and Madres de Plaza Línea Fundadora
May 14, 1989	Carlos Saúl Menem elected
1989 and 1990	Menem pardons all charged and convicted of Dirty War crimes
1995	military officers confess crimes; Mothers continue to march

Further Reading

Amnesty International. *Argentina, The Military Juntas and Human Rights*. London, England: Amnesty International Publications, 1987. Provides some background information on human rights abuses in Argentina and the attempt to bring the abusers to trial.

Gofen, Ethel Caro. *Cultures of the World—Argentina*. New York: Marshall Cavendish, 1991. Part of a series for young people on the nations of the world. This title contains a brief history of the Dirty War and the return to democracy in Argentina.

Gray, Paul. "Waves from the Past." *Time* magazine. March 27, 1995, p. 45. A former member of the navy describes atrocities committed by the military in 1977. Includes photo of the Mothers of the Plaza.

Simpson, John and Jana Bennett. *The Disappeared and the Mothers of the Plaza*. New York: St. Martin's Press. 1985. A History of the Dirty War in Argentina including a detailed account of the activities of the Mothers of the Plaza.

Chinese physicist Fang Lizhi, now a professor in the United States, was among those blamed for "inciting students" to call for democratic reform in China in the 1980s. (Courtesy Fang Lizhi)

Fang Lizhi

CHINESE DEMOCRACY
MOVEMENT ACTIVIST
(1936–   )

It was unlike anything the city of Hefei, China, had ever seen. Thousands of students marched from the campus of the Chinese University of Science and Technology into the streets of the capital of Anhui province. Some carried signs featuring the American Statue of Liberty. Others chose quotations from Americans such as Abraham Lincoln ("government of the people, by the people and for the people") and Patrick Henry ("Give me liberty or give me death"). Some posted signs on the walls of buildings they passed calling for democracy in China.

Word of the student demonstrations in Hefei on December 5, 1986, spread to other cities in China, especially to other campuses. Demonstrations attracted thousands of students in Wuhan, a provincial capital west of Hefei, and Shanghai. Chinese officials, priding themselves on maintaining order, decided that something had to be done. These protests, though nonviolent, were decidedly "unorderly."

It was not hard to find a scapegoat. An astrophysicist at the University of Science and Technology, and a vice president of the university, had made numerous speeches about "democracy" and "freedom of expression." He must be the one to blame for inciting the students. His name was Fang Lizhi.

Fang Lizhi was born February 12, 1936, in Beijing, China. At the time, China was torn by a civil war between Nationalists and Communists, as well as fighting against invading Japanese forces. After the Japanese were driven from China, the civil war intensified, ending in a victory for the Communists. Their leader, Mao Zedong, proclaimed the People's Republic of China on October 1, 1949.

It was in this Communist-ruled China that sixteen-year-old Fang Lizhi entered Beijing University in 1952. A brilliant student, he studied theoretical and nuclear physics, and graduated in 1956. In 1953, he had his first confrontation with the Communist Party about his tendency to speak his mind. During one of its frequent persecutions of intellectuals, the party expelled him.

Fang was a promising young scientist, however, and in 1958 he became an assistant teacher at the University of Science and Technology. In 1961, he married a fellow physicist, Li Shuxian, who he met in college. He was promoted to lecturer in 1963, but in 1966 he was again the victim of anti-intellectuals, this time during the so-called Cultural Revolution. This was a turbulent time in China during which radicals in the Communist party seized control of local and provincial governments and closed down schools and universities. While being forced to work in the countryside as a peasant, Fang refused to give up his right to think, repeatedly reading the one book he'd managed to keep. He later said that during this time he still believed in communism, but was beginning to doubt Mao's leadership.

By 1971 he was considered sufficiently "rehabilitated" to regain teaching privileges at the University of Science and Technology. In 1976, he was teaching in Hefei, when Mao Zedong died. In the struggle for power that followed, a new leader, Deng Xiaoping, emerged. Deng promoted reforms that improved China's relations with the West—but Deng was much more cautious about political than economic reform.

Inevitably, changes in the government raised questions and concerns among the people. During the winter of 1978–79, "big character posters" began to appear on a brick wall in central Beijing later known as the Democracy Wall. One poster placed there by 28-year-old Wei Jingsheng was entitled the "Fifth Modernization." Wei claimed that China's Four Modernization goals (agricultural, industrial, scientific and military improvements) would be meaningless without a fifth goal—democracy. On his poster Wei wrote that when people demanded democracy, "they are only asking for something they rightfully own."

Deng Xiaoping disagreed. On March 29, 1979, Wei Jingsheng was arrested and charged with "counterrevolutionary" activities and with disclosing state military secrets. At his trial, Wei stated, "It is the right of every citizen to criticize any unreasonable people or thing that he sees." Found guilty he was sentenced to 15 years in prison.

Countless others who dared to dissent were arrested, and the majority of Chinese intellectuals learned to keep their opinions to themselves. One of the few who continued to speak up was Fang Lizhi.

Fang had had his party membership restored in 1978 and and in 1984 he became vice president of the University of Science and Technology. He was able to take advantage of the government's openness toward the West, and traveled to scientific conferences in Europe and the United States. Fang became one of only a very few Chinese scientists with an international reputation for his research of laser theory and black holes.

As time went on, Fang Lizhi became as well known for his writings on human rights as for those on science. He said that as a scientist, he was trained to study the facts to learn the truth. When forced to choose between truth and what the Communisty Party taught, he chose truth. The truth was that "every individual possesses human rights and human rights are very basic."

This was the truth that he delivered to the students when he lectured on various campuses in China. Fang described the corruption he saw in the Communist Party, and urged the students to pursue democracy.

When the students took to the streets in December of 1986, Deng Xiaoping blamed intellectuals, and especially Fang Lizhi, for the unrest. Deng charged that it was Fang Lizhi's words that had given the students their dangerous notions. On January 12, 1987, Fang was fired from the vice presidency of the Science and Technology Institute; he was also expelled from the Communist Party. He was "transferred" to the position of researcher at Beijing Observatory. Students were required by the government to read Fang's writings, in the hope that they would find them foolish. This, however, had the opposite effect. Now more students than ever began to support Fang's human rights stance. To many of the students, Fang became a hero.

Fang Lizhi continued to pursue his career at the Beijing Observatory of Beijing University. Beijing Observatory noted that he had more scientific articles published in 1988 than any other researcher at the university. However, Fang was forbidden to speak to foreign reporters; Chinese

> "Human rights aren't the property of a particular race or nationality. Every human being has from birth the right to live, to think, to speak, to find a mate. These are the most fundamental freedoms a human being has. Every person on the surface of the earth should have these rights, regardless of what country he lives in."
>
> —Fang Lizhi, quoted in *The Broken Mirror* by George Hicks

reporters were forbidden to quote him directly. On at least one occasion, a lecture hall in which he was supposed to speak was locked and guarded by police to prevent students from hearing his message.

Fang was allowed to travel to a scientific conference in Italy, but when he spoke about democracy to reporters there, he was ordered by the Chinese government to return home. He was not allowed to travel to England or the United States, despite numerous invitations from scientific organizations. Fang said to an American friend, "I have eight invitations, all entirely non-political. I have [been given by the government] three reasons for denial, all entirely political."

Fang continued to make his voice heard. In interviews and speeches, he criticized the Chinese government's denial of human rights, and called for an end to one-party rule. "I'm a soldier who already crossed the river," he said when asked if he was afraid of being arrested. "There's no way to turn back."

On January 6, 1989, Fang wrote an open letter to Deng Xiaoping, asking for a general amnesty for political prisoners in honor of the upcoming 40th anniversary of the founding of the People's Republic, and in particular, for the release of Wei Jingsheng, then in the 10th year of his 15-year-sentence. Fang also noted that 1989 marked the 200th anniversary of the French Revolution, whose motto "Liberty, Equality, Fraternity" had played a significant role. Thirty-three other Chinese intellectuals followed Fang's example with letters of their own, repeating the call for the release of political prisoners.

At about the same time, an article by Fang Lizhi entitled "China Needs Democracy" was published in a French newspaper. In this article, Fang made such statements as "Not only have the forty years of Maoist China been a failure but even the past ten 'years of reform' have produced nothing to justify a chorus of praise." Fang went so far as to say, "Socialism, in its Lenin-Stalin-Mao version, has been entirely discredited."

In a speech later in January, Fang said that pressure should be placed on the government, but insisted that "this pressure is not intended to overthrow anybody. We only want to pressure people to go in the right direction."

In February, the recently inaugurated U.S. president, George Bush, former liaison to China, paid Deng a "goodwill" visit. This goodwill evaporated on February 26, when Fang Lizhi was prevented by police from attending a barbecue hosted by Bush. As an American colleague described it, "Fang and [his wife] Li were humiliatingly tailed through the cold streets of Beijing by bevies of police and repeatedly prevented not only from riding in cars but even from boarding public buses."

The Chinese government said it was disrespectful of the United States to have invited Fang Lizhi. Fang's response was, " . . . it's a good example of the state of human rights in China. Not just my rights [were violated], also my wife's rights, also my American friends', also many ordinary people who were waiting for the bus. They could not get home. Their rights were violated."

On April 5, Li Shuxian, professor of physics and wife of Fang Lizhi, spoke about democratic reform to a crowd of nearly 250 students at Beijing University. One of the students was Wang Dan, a 20-year-old history major. Wang started a discussion group where students could meet to talk about democracy and human rights. "We're just trying to create an atmosphere where people can discover things," he said. Within the next few weeks, as students marched from the university, he would be one of the leaders.

The spark that set off the protests was the death on April 15, 1989, of Communist leader Hu Yaobang, whom the students believed was sympathetic to their cause. On April 17, thousands of students marched to the monument to Communist martyrs in Tiananmen Square, a popular gathering place in Beijing. Students continued to demonstrate

In April 1989, students took to the streets, leading to a violent reprisal by the government in Tiananmen Square. With a banner strapped to its grill saying, "Long Live the Students!" a truck speeds through Beijing carrying prodemocracy protesters. (Courtesy Retuers/Bettmann)

during the next several days. On Saturday, April 22, roughly 150,000 people, mostly students, gathered in the square on the day of the official funeral service of Hu Yaobang.

For the next several weeks, the students continued to occupy the square. They set up tents and made arrangements for garbage removal and water delivery. They used loudspeakers and posters to express their demands for democracy, human rights, and freedom of the press.

As a long-planned meeting between Soviet Premier Mikhail Gorbachev and Deng Xiaoping grew closer, the Chinese leaders grew more concerned about the demonstrations in the square. The meeting was supposed to mark the beginning of improved relations between the two large Communist nations. When Gorbachev arrived in China on May 15, some 3,000 students on a hunger strike were lying on the street in Tiananmen Square. They were surrounded by tens of thousands of other students and curious spectators. Day by day, more students poured into the city from around the country. As many as a million citizens participated at various times in demonstrations in and around the square during April and May. To the great embarrassment of Chinese officials, many of the ceremonies planned for the Gorbachev visit had to be canceled or moved because of the demonstrations.

On May 19, as the students prepared to end the hunger strike, government officials prepared for

"The fact that the violent suppression of peaceful demonstrators was deliberate, not an accident of war or a riot out of control, and was ordered by China's leaders and carried out by China's People's Liberation Army compounds the crime."

—Donald and Constance Shanor, in *China Today*

military measures to restore order. The next morning, martial law went into effect in central Beijing. All "destructive actions," including boycotting classes and giving speeches, were banned.

As troops gathered around the city, the people of Beijing took to the streets to show support for the students, and interfere with troop movements. They lectured the soldiers about democracy and told them to go home. In fact, many of the students were going home, or at least back to school. The movement seemed to be losing some of its momentum.

Then, on May 30 students from the Central Fine Arts Academy unveiled their "Goddess of Democracy," a 33-foot-tall statue of a woman in classical Grecian dress holding a torch, reminiscent of the American Statue of Liberty. The statue brought people back to the square and gave the demonstration new life.

That was the last straw for the government. On June 3, the troops that had gathered around Beijing began advancing steadily toward Tiananmen Square. In the early hours of June 4, hundreds of people were killed as soldiers fired on demonstrators and bystanders. Some soldiers were killed by citizens who fought back, trying to stop the troops from reaching the square.

It was said that students who left the square in one direction were able to escape unharmed, but that a large group who left another way were mowed down by machine-gun fire. As tanks rolled through the square, they crushed the Goddess of Democracy, the students' tents, and any students who may have been sleeping or hiding in those tents.

In the streets people were shouting "Many are dead, many are dead." "My government has gone crazy," said a blood-stained doctor, trying to help the injured. The government-controlled media reported that the People's Army had "suppressed a counterrevolutionary riot."

We will probably never know exactly how many people died on June 3, 4, and 5 in China. A government spokesman put the number at 300. An Amnesty International report estimated that 1,000 people died. The actual number may be even higher.

The government asked citizens to report those who'd been involved in the "hooliganism and destruction." At least 4,000 people were arrested, including student leader Wang Dan. A man who was seen telling an American television crew that 20,000 people had been killed in the military attack on the square was sentenced to ten years in prison. Life in prison was the sentence given to a high-school teacher who splashed paint on a portrait of Mao. Still others were sentenced to death; sentences were carried out immediately.

A number of Western nations imposed economic penalties on China. The U.S. Congress condemned the actions of the Chinese government and moved to link the prized "most favored nation" trading status with human rights improvement. The American government also wanted to make it easier for Chinese students already in the United States to remain.

China, angered by the criticism, stated that "China was the victim," of the demonstrators. Deng Xiaoping congratulated the army for saving China from the dangerous "hooligans."

> "Tiananmen cannot simply be forgotten. The massacre of hundreds of Chinese democracy demonstrators, including scores of students, and the wounding or imprisonment of thousands of others is a political crime whose resolution must await the change of leadership in China.
>
> —Donald and Constance Shanor, in *China Today*

Fang Lizhi stayed away from the square during the demonstrations. He knew the students were speaking for themselves, and did not want the government to be able to claim that he organized them. As the government crackdown on the demonstrators increased, Fang and his wife sought shelter in the U.S. embassy, fearing, correctly, that there were warrants for their arrest.

While hidden in the embassy for over a year, Fang tried to continue his work. He and his wife could not go outside, and spent most of their days in two rooms with boarded-up windows and locked doors for their protection. Even when Fang was named the recipient of the 1989 Robert F. Kennedy Human Rights award, he remained hidden from sight from all but a few embassy staff members. On June 25, 1990, Fang and Li were finally able to leave China, first for Britain, and then for the United States. Fang Lizhi became a professor of physics at the University of Arizona.

For the next several years, the Chinese government retained its strict control against internal criticism. In March 1993, as China sought to improve its reputation in hopes of gaining the right to host the Olympic Games in the year 2000, student leader Wang Dan was released from police custody. Wei Jingsheng was released after 14 years in the Chinese prison system. These attempts seemed superficial, however, as Wei Jingsheng was again apprehended in 1994 for continuing to promote human rights and democracy. In 1995, American Harry Wu was captured by Chinese security agents while trying to examine human rights violations in China. Wu was released on the eve of a huge United Nations–sponsored international women's conference in Beijing, during which many women participants complained of being harassed by Chinese police and plain-clothes security officers.

Once, when asked how democracy could be implemented in China, Fang answered, "I think we should start with respect for the basic human rights. If we have the freedoms of thought, expression, and assembly, we can gradually move toward a full democratic system. But it will take time. I don't know if I can see it in my lifetime."

Chronology

February 12, 1936	born in Beijing, China
October 1, 1949	Chinese Communists defeat Chinese Nationalists; the People's Republic of China is born
1961	Fang Lizhi marries Li Shuxian
1966	arrested during the Cultural Revolution; sent to countryside as a forced laborer
1978–1979	Democracy Wall posters hung; Wei Jingsheng arrested
1984	Fang Lizhi becomes vice president of University of Science and Technology
December 1986	student protests erupt on many campuses
January 1987	Fang Lizhi fired as university vice president and expelled from Communist Party
January 6, 1989	open letter to Deng Xiaoping
February 26, 1989	prevented from attending banquet given by President George Bush in China
April 15, 1989	death of moderate leader Hu Yaobang sets off student protests in Beijing
May 15–18	Chinese leader Deng Xiaoping is embarrassed by student demonstrations during Soviet leader Mikhail Gorbachev visit
May 20	martial law declared in Beijing
May 30	Goddess of Democracy statue is raised in Tiananmen Square

June 3–5, 1989	military crackdown on demonstrators results in hundreds of deaths; Fang Lizhi seeks asylum in U.S. embassy
October, 1989	awarded the Robert F. Kennedy Human Rights award
June 25, 1990	Fang Lizhi and Li Shuxian allowed to leave China for exile in the West
1993	student leader Wang Dan and Democracy Wall protester Wei Jingsheng released
1995	American human rights investigator Harry Wu arrested in China, released before international women's conference

Further Reading

Carter, Alden R. *China Past—China Future.* New York: Franklin Watts, 1994. A history of China, written for young people, which includes a look at present conditions and outlook for the future.

Gargan, Edward A. *China's Fate, A People's Turbulent Struggle with Reform and Repression, 1980–1990.* New York: Doubleday, 1990. Interesting and detailed history of events leading to and including the Tiananmen Square Massacre.

Human Rights in China. Children of the Dragon, The Story of Tiananmen Square. New York: Collier Books, 1990. With extensive use of photographs, chronicles the turbulent days of spring, 1989 in Beijing. Includes a postscript by Fang Lizhi.

Schell, Orville. "China's Andrei Sakharov." *The Atlantic Monthly.* May, 1988, p. 35–52. Article which traces the involvement of Fang Lizhi in the democratic reform movement in China.

Simmie, Scott and Bob Nixon. *Tiananmen Square.* Seattle: University of Washington Press, 1989. Eyewitness account of the Chinese student demonstrations with biographical information about Fang Lizhi.

Joan Baez attained fame as a folksinger and used her resources to fight for human rights around the world. (Courtesy Joan Baez, photo by Dan Borris)

Joan Baez

VOICE FOR HUMANITY
(1941–   )

It was Christmas Eve, 1972, and the sounds of falling bombs crashed through the night. Huddled in the bomb shelter of a hotel in Hanoi, the capital of North Vietnam, were a number of Vietnamese citizens and a handful of foreigners, including four Americans. One was a lawyer, another a minister, the third a Vietnam veteran, and the fourth was a folk singer/human rights activist. The group had been invited by the Committee for Solidarity with the American People, a North Vietnamese group that hoped they could encourage Americans to demand an end to the war. They would witness the destruction that U.S. bombing had caused in North Vietnam, deliver mail to U.S. prisoners of war, and be home before Christmas. At least, that was their plan.

Unknown to them, the U.S. government had another plan. In order to force the North Vietnamese back to the peace conferences, the government planned to initiate a heavy bombing attack on Hanoi. When it was over, it would be known as the heaviest bombing in the history of the world. The bombing began on the group's third night in Hanoi. Shortly after dinner, the lights in the hotel went out, and air raid sirens went off. Everyone in the hotel was sent down to a bomb shelter. When the raid was over, they went back to bed, only a short while later to have their sleep interrupted by more sirens and then more bombs. Before that night was over, there were ten raids. Over the next several days the raids fell into a pattern, one at noon, one in mid-afternoon, and many during the night. When the group went out during the day, they saw the ruins of the buildings, the bomb craters, and the dead.

Since the airport had been bombed and the runways damaged, they could not leave before Christmas. On Christmas Eve, the folk singer got out her guitar and sang a Christmas carol and the Lord's Prayer. Before she could finish, the lights went out, the sirens blared, and the bombs came again.

It was New Year's Day when the folksinger, Joan Baez, finally arrived home. From her memories and the tapes she'd made, she put together an album she dedicated to the Vietnamese people. The name of the album is *Where Are You Now, My Son?* An avowed pacifist well before that terrible Christmas, she was now more committed than ever to the support of nonviolence.

Joan Baez was born in Staten Island, New York, on January 9, 1941. Her father, Albert Baez, was born in Mexico but came to the United States as a child. Her mother, Joan Bridge, was born in Scotland but raised in the United States. Eventually, the couple had three daughters: Pauline, Joan, and Mimi.

While Joan was still very young, her family moved to California, where her father studied advanced physics. After receiving his Ph.D., Albert Baez got a job at Cornell University in Ithaca, New York, and once again the family moved across the country. A short while later they would be back in California after Albert changed jobs again.

In 1951, the family moved to Baghdad, Iraq, when Albert's work took him there. In her memoirs, Joan writes,

> Perhaps that was where my passion for social justice was born. The day we landed, in the heat and the strange new smells, we were horrified to see an old beggar being driven out of the airport gates by policemen. . . . I saw animals beaten to death, people rooting for food in our family garbage pails, and legless children dragging themselves along the streets on cardboard, covered with flies feasting on open sores, begging for money.

After a year, the family returned to California, where Joan attended junior high school. Her background and unique experiences made her different from many of the other students; she sometimes found it difficult to fit in. Joan did not let this stop her from taking a stand against discrimination and nuclear war.

When she was a junior in high school, Joan attended a three-day conference on world issues sponsored by the American Friends Service Committee. The main speaker was a 27-year-old black preacher from Alabama—Martin Luther King, Jr. "He talked about injustice and suffering," she recalled "and about fighting with the weapons of love, saying that when someone does evil to us, we can hate the evil deed but not the doer of the deed, who is to be pitied. He talked about organizing a nonviolent revolution. When he finished his speech, I was on my feet, cheering and crying."

Shortly after, she met a Quaker named Ira Sandperl. She described Ira as "a Mahatma Gandhi scholar, an advocate of radical nonviolent

"Martin Luther King, Jr., more than any other public figure helped to solidify my ideas and inspired me to act on them."

—Joan Baez, *And A Voice to Sing With*

change." The things Ira told her about fighting evil with the weapons of nonviolence made sense to Joan.

After she finished high school, the Baez family moved to Boston. Joan planned to attend the Boston University School of Drama, but she found sitting around coffeehouses, listening to folk music more interesting. She also liked to sing, and soon *she* was one of the singers that people were listening to as she performed in coffeehouses for $10 a night. She soon dropped out of school.

In 1959, Joan was invited to sing at the Newport Folk Festival in Rhode Island, and was a big hit. She continued to perform and develop her own style of singing ballads, spirituals, and folk songs from around the world. Joan made her first record in 1960, and in 1961 went on her first concert tour around the United States.

In 1962, Joan performed at a fund-raiser for the civil rights movement, a cause in which she firmly believed. Later that summer, at the same time that Martin Luther King, Jr., was leading a civil rights protest in that city, she sang at an all-black college in Birmingham, Alabama. To show her support for the demonstrators, Baez closed her concert with the protest song "We Shall Overcome." The audience joined in, holding hands and crying.

Besides the civil rights movement, there was another cause that greatly concerned Joan Baez. During the Kennedy presidency, the American government had begun sending an increasing number of "military advisers" to a small Asian country, South Vietnam. In late 1963, only weeks after Lyndon Johnson became president of the United States following the assassination of John F. Kennedy, Baez sang at a White House concert. Before singing one of her songs, she looked straight at President Johnson and told him that America's youth did not want to fight in Vietnam.

Within the next year, American involvement in Vietnam increased, and Baez decided to withold the portion of her income tax that she estimated would go to the military. The government eventually collected the money, and fined her. But the Internal Revenue Service had to work to get the money, and Baez felt that she had made her point by not giving it to them.

In 1965, with her friend Ira Sandperl, Baez cofounded the Institute for the Study of Nonviolence in Carmel Valley, California. Of the institute, she said, "we studied the concept, theory, history and application of nonviolence in all its aspects."

Joan continued to protest the escalating war in Vietnam. In October 1967, she was arrested for interfering at a draft induction center. Months later she was arrested again for similar actions, and met David Harris, a leader of the draft resistance. He shared her interest in nonviolence and concern for victims of war. They began working together, fell in love, and were married March 26, 1968. They lived in a commune with other draft resisters at Struggle Mountain. Joan had recently discovered she was pregnant when David was taken to federal prison on July 16, 1969 for refusing induction into the army. She was six months pregnant when she sang at the Woodstock music festival and spoke about her husband's stand against the war that sent him to prison. Harris was released from prison March 15, 1971, ten months after their son Gabriel was born. After the long separation, it proved impossible for the couple to rebuild a life together; they separated in 1972 and were divorced the following year.

Baez and Harris shared responsibility for raising their son, and Joan was able to continue with her work. In the spring of 1972 she organized the Ring Around Congress—women holding hands in Washington—to show solidarity with the women and children of Vietnam. Some 2,500 women listened to speeches, sang songs, and demanded an end to the war. In December she was in Hanoi during the Christmas bombing. That bombing came to a halt in mid-January, and on January 27, 1973, a treaty was signed in Paris that called for the withdrawal of U.S. troops from Vietnam.

By then, Baez was busily involved in organizing a West Coast branch of Amnesty International, an organization working for the release of people imprisoned for religious or political beliefs. The year before, she met Ginetta Sagan, an Italian woman imprisoned and tortured by Nazis during World War II. Ginetta told Joan about Amnesty, and together they told others. At concerts, Baez handed out pamphlets with the names and addresses of political prisoners and those to write to to demand their release. Baez went to demonstrations against the death penalty and gave benefit concerts for political prisoners. She became more aware of human rights abuses around the world and continued to look for ways to use her singing for the benefit of humanity. Joan sang to support the Mothers of the Plaza de Mayo in Argentina; she sang over the telephone to Russian dissidents Andrei Sakharov and Elena Bonner.

One quiet morning in 1979, as Baez remembered it, she was visited by two refugees from Vietnam. Since the American troops had pulled out of South Vietnam, the North Vietnamese had moved in and unified the country. The two refugees told Baez horror stories of human rights violations in the now Communist-controlled country. They asked her to help.

Baez and her friend Ginetta Sagan formed a group to study the situation. In the past, Baez had been criticized by conservative right-wing politicians for her opposition to U.S. activities in Vietnam. Now the political left would be angered by her criticism of the Communist regime, but Baez did not tailor her actions to please any particular political group.

Joan wrote an open letter to the Socialist Republic of Vietnam, and collected 81 signatures to add to her own. In it she wrote:

Baez met with President Carter in the White House to share concerns about human rights. (Courtesy Jimmy Carter Library)

It was an abiding commitment to fundamental principles of human dignity, freedom, and self-determination that motivated so many Americans to oppose the government of South Vietnam and our country's participation in the war. It is that same commitment that compels us to speak out against your brutal disregard of human rights. As in the 60s, we raise our voices now so that your people may live.

The letter was printed as a paid advertisement in the *New York Times*, the *Washington Post*, the *Los Angeles Times*, and the *San Francisco Chronicle*. Baez and other supporters were encouraged when many prisoners were released in Vietnam, though she noted sadly that the situation there remains grim.

Next, Baez focused on the plight of the 15 million refugees from the brutal actions of Cambodian Communists, the Khmer Rouge, and the invasion of Cambodia by Vietnam. On July 19, 1979, she organized a concert at the Lincoln Memorial followed by a candlelit march to the White House as a show of support for help to the boat people, refugees who attempted to flee Cambodia for Thailand by boat across the South China Sea. It was attended by about 10,000 people. President Carter, committed to the support of human rights, personally appeared at the White House gates to announce that he would send the Sixth Fleet to the South China Sea. The next morning, Carter telephoned Baez, and they congratulated each other on the humanitarian effort that would be made. In October 1979, the president's son Chip stood by Joan all evening at a fund-raiser for the boat people in Washington D. C.

Still, she wanted to do more. Joan decided to go to Thailand to visit the refugee camps. There, she could sing for the people and gain attention for their plight. She and a friend took a train from Bangkok to northern Thailand, and drove to a refugee camp along a river at the border between Thailand and Laos. When they reached the camp they learned that a group of Laotians had swum across the river and were nearing shore. They also heard that the Thai border patrol might send the refugees back or shoot them.

Baez immediately went to see the colonel in charge of the camp. She pleaded with him to let the refugees in. "Whatever kind of man you are on other days, why not be a man of God today and give the lives back to those miserable souls at the river," she said, adding, "I am concerned enough to get down on my knees before you and beg for their lives," which she did.

"When I hear that all those people are safely ashore," she said, "I will sing a very special concert, and dedicate a song to you." She walked off with knees shaking, but it worked. The refugees that made it to shore were allowed to stay.

In that camp and others, Baez sang her heart out for the refugees, especially for the children. For them she sang "I Love My Rooster," pleased to be able to make them smile in the midst of the horror that surrounded them. In camp after camp, she would remember, "The children were always there, defying pain, defying death, defying hopelessness. The children, always ready for a tomorrow, even when all was lost."

At one camp she saw a boy lying by the road, starving and ill. "Who can get this kid to a hospital?" she asked. An American photographer picked up the boy and carried him past Thai soldiers who pointed their guns at him, saying, "This little boy is very sick. I'm taking him to the hospital." Later, the photographer returned to say that the boy had been safely delivered to a hospital and was being given good food.

The study group Baez had formed in 1979 grew into a human rights organization named Humanitas/International Human Rights Committee. Baez and the staff she gathered continued to monitor human rights situations around the world. They protested the U.S. bombing of Libya and intervention in Nicaragua, and supported Bishop Tutu's nonviolent actions in South Africa. "We managed to return Irina Grunina, a Russian dissident in exile, to Moscow for proper health care in time for the birth of her baby," Baez reported happily.

"I am proud of what Humanitas has accomplished since its inception in 1979," she says. "Although I cannot always work closely with it on each and every project, it gives me great comfort to know that Humanitas is still constantly at work on the issues that are so important to me.

Baez was touched by the hope she saw in the faces of refugee children she sang to in Thailand. (Courtesy Jimmy Carter Library)

Baez never seemed to run out of causes to sing for. On June 16, 1982, she sang for Peace Sunday before 90,000 people in Pasadena, California. Nearly a million people heard her sing the following week in New York City's Central Park at an anti-nuclear rally. On July 13, 1985, she opened the Live Aid concert with "Amazing Grace" and "We Are the World." Live Aid was televised around the world and featured numerous performers singing both from London and Philadelphia. The concert's purpose was to raise money for the world's hungry.

Amnesty International agreed with Baez and others that music is an effective way to reach people, and raise funds. In 1986 Amnesty organized a concert tour called Conspiracy of Hope to celebrate its 25th anniversary and raise awareness about human rights abuses. Joan Baez was among the prominent performers.

In 1992 she released a new album, *Play Me Backwards*. After producing more than 30 albums in the 30 years since 1960, she proved that she still had the voice and the songs to sing. In 1993, she went on tour in the United States to promote the album, but interrupted the tour in April 1993, to sing in Sarajevo and Zagreb, cities rent by war in the former Yugoslavia. Baez later said that during her performances, "You could hear shelling and you knew how vital it was that you just kept on going." Of Sarajevo she said, "There was not one building or car I saw that didn't have bullet holes in it."

"Through all these changes my social and political views have remained astoundingly steadfast. I have been true to the principles of nonviolence, developing a stronger and stronger aversion to the ideologies of both the far right and the far left and a deeper sense of rage and sorrow over the suffering they continue to produce all over the world."

—Joan Baez, *And a Voice to Sing With*

Though Humanitas/International was forced to close its doors officially in August 1992 due to financial difficulties, Joan Baez still works as a human rights activist. Part of the reason she carries on this work is explained in an interview conducted in 1970 wherein, responding to the question, what if the nonviolent revolution never happens, she said,

> Well, I want to have lived my life in such a way that I won't regret any of the things I've done. So even if we never reach the goal, I'll at least have attempted to live a decent life all the way through. I'll have kept on trying to reach people, trying to keep myself open, so that *I* can be reached, trying to be kind, trying to learn about love. In my most down moments, I think maybe that will be the most we'll be able to do—to live a life of *trying* to do those things. And if it comes to that, it will, after all, have been quite a lot to have done.

Chronology

January 9, 1941	Joan Baez born, Staten Island, New York
July 1959	performs at Newport Folk Festival
1965	cofounds Institute for the Study of Nonviolence
1967	arrested for anti-war protest
March 26, 1968	marries draft-resistance leader David Harris
July 16, 1969	Harris begins serving nearly two years in prison for draft resistance
1972	Baez separates from Harris, organizes "Ring Around the Congress" protest, spends Christmas in Hanoi during heavy U.S. bombing

1973	organizes West Coast branch of Amnesty International
1979	organizes study group which becomes Humanitas/International Human Rights Committee, sends open letter to government of Vietnam, holds a concert for the boat people, goes to Thailand
July 13, 1985	sings at Live Aid concert
1986	sings at Conspiracy of Hope concert
April 1993	sings in former Yugoslavia

Further Reading

Baez, Joan. *And a Voice to Sing With*. New York: Summit Books, 1987. Baez's autobiography, including her human rights work.

Duffy, Thom. "Baez Performs in 2 War-torn ex-Yugo Cities." *Billboard*, May 1, 1993. p 10. Short article that includes comments Baez made after visiting cities in Bosnia.

Garza, Hedda. *Joan Baez*. New York: Chelsea House, 1991. Biography for young people. Includes photos.

Aung San Suu Kyi, daughter of a martyred Burmese leader, was held under house arrest for six years for protesting government abuse of human rights in Burma. (Courtesy *The Burma Review*, photo by Sandro Tucci: Black Star)

Aung San Suu Kyi

ICON OF HOPE FOR BURMA
(1945–)

People began gathering near the Shwedagon Pagoda in Rangoon, the capital of Myanmar (previously known as Burma), on the afternoon of August 25th, 1988. They prepared their evening meal and lay down to sleep on their bedrolls. They wanted to have a good spot to hear the speech that would be made the next day.

On August 26, some 500,000 people were gathered, including the very young and the very old. Members of Burma's many ethnic groups were represented in the crowd, and people from all walks of life could be seen. Students and monks formed human chains around the stage where the guest speaker would soon stand. At last she arrived, her car left some distance from the stage because of the huge throng. As she made her way up to the stage she could see the enormous portrait of Burmese hero General Aung San that hung there. It was a familiar face, though General Aung San had died when she was very young. General Aung San was her father; her name was Aung San Suu Kyi.

Aung San Suu Kyi was born June 19, 1945, in Rangoon, the capital of Burma. Since 1885, the ancient kingdom of Burma had been a British colony; that was about to end. The Burma

Independence Army, led by General Aung San, fought both the Japanese and British during World War II in an effort to win independence. Just as that independence was about to be achieved, General Aung San was assassinated on July 19, 1947, by followers of a political rival. Only 32 years old when he died, he would be remembered as a hero by the Burmese people. On January 4, 1948, Burma became an independent republic.

In addition to his two-year-old daughter, Aung San left two sons, Aung San Oo and Aung San Lin, but sadly, the younger son Lin died in a drowning accident. Bravely, their mother, Daw Khin Kyi, continued the work of her husband as a member of Burma's Parliament, resigning to become director of the Children and Mothers Welfare Board. This work led her to other service positions, and offered her the opportunity to travel to other parts of Asia and the world.

Daw Khin Kyi became Burmese ambassador to India when Suu Kyi was 15. Suu Kyi happily traveled with her, and completed her schooling in India. She learned about and developed an appreciation for the principles of nonviolence taught by the great Indian leader Mohandas Gandhi. Suu Kyi worked hard and was always one of the best students in her class, but there was time for recreation too. Her mother enrolled her in riding lessons with the children of other diplomats, and the grandchildren of Indian Prime Minister Jawaharlal Nehru. Always she was reminded of her father, who had consulted with Nehru. Nearly every 19th of July, she returned to Burma with her mother for the observance of Martyr's Day, when her father and others were mourned and remembered.

In 1964, Aung San Suu Kyi traveled to England to attend St. Hugh's College, Oxford. She studied philosophy, politics, and economics, and graduated in 1967. At that time a Burmese leader, U Thant, was Secretary General of the

United Nations, which probably inspired Suu Kyi to seek work there. She moved to New York City, got an apartment, and went to work as an information officer for the United Nations. In her spare time, she volunteered at Bellevue Hospital, a place for the city's poor suffering from physical and mental problems.

The years Aung San Suu Kyi spent abroad had been difficult ones for her homeland. In 1962, a military takeover led by General Ne Win resulted in a government of only one political party, Ne Win's Burmese Socialist Program Party. No opposition to that party would be allowed, as Ne Win proved in July 1962 when soldiers opened fire on students on a university campus. As Bertil Lintner reports in his book *Outrage*, "Officially, 15 were killed and 27 wounded. But both neutral observers and students who were present during the shooting say that the university looked like a slaughter-house where not 15 but hundreds of potential leaders of society lay sprawled in death."

As Ne Win ruled Burma with a heavy hand, Suu Kyi made decisions that determined the course of her life. On January 1, 1972, she married Michael Aris, a British scholar she met at Oxford. Aris was employed in Bhutan as a private tutor to that small Himalayan country's royal family. Daw Aung San Suu Kyi ("Daw" is a title of respect for an adult woman, somewhat like "Mrs.") worked in Bhutan's Foreign Ministry, and advised the government on United Nations affairs.

The couple was very happy, but Aung San Suu Kyi foresaw that the day might come when her devotion

> "This struggle is between a handful of military men and the entire population of Burma—people who are literally starving for freedom."
>
> —National League for Democracy leader, quoted in *Burma: The Next Killing Fields?*

During the spring of 1988, student demonstrators in Rangoon called for multiparty elections and other democratic reforms. They are carrying the national flag, student banners and portraits of General Aung San. (Reuters/Bettman Courtesy Bettmann Archives)

to her homeland might make things difficult. Before their marriage, she wrote to Michael, "I only ask one thing, that should my people need me, you would help me to do my duty by them."

In 1973, they moved to Oxford, England. There they had two sons, Myint San Aung (also known as Alexander) and Htein Lin (Kim).

During the following years, Aung San Suu Kyi regularly visited Rangoon to see her mother and to do research on her father and his work. She made sure that her sons were brought up with an understanding of their Burmese heritage. She taught for a while at a university in Japan, and later continued her own studies in India. In April 1988, she had just begun work on her post-graduate thesis in London, when she received word that her mother suffered a stroke.

Immediately she traveled to Burma; she cared for her mother in the hospital until she was able to bring her to the family home in July, when she was joined by her husband and sons.

The spring of 1988 was an explosive time in Burma. For some months students had been demonstrating, calling for a multiparty general election. Hundreds of students had been arrested and some were killed by government forces. Students released from government detention told horrific tales of torture and rape. Security officers wanted to pinpoint the movement's organizers. They did not believe such demonstrations could have been a spontaneous response to years of injustice. The demonstrations and government reprisals continued into the summer months. Hundreds of thousands of students, monks, and ordinary citizens marched for democracy in Rangoon and other places. According to one report, between August 8th and 12th at least 1,000 people were killed in the army's response to these marches.

Aung San Suu Kyi watched these developments with horror as she cared for her ailing mother. She had always kept her Burmese citizenship, and gradually came to realize that as her father's daughter, it was impossible for her to remain quiet any longer. On August 15 she sent a letter to the government asking that a committee be formed to deal with the crisis.

"Within a system which denies the existence of basic human rights, fear tends to be the order of the day. Fear of imprisonment, fear of torture, fear of death, fear of losing friends, family, property. . . . Yet even under the most crushing state machinery courage rises up again and again, for fear is not the natural state of civilized man."

—Aung San Suu Kyi,
Freedom from Fear

When her letter was not answered, she arranged to speak at the rally on August 26. As she stood on a stage below a portrait of her father, she said that though 40 years had passed since Burma had won its independence from Britain, its people were now engaged in a "second struggle for national independence." She continued:

> A number of people are saying that since I've spent most of my life abroad and am married to a foreigner, I could not be familiar with the ramifications of this country's politics. But these facts have never, and will never interfere with or lessen my love and devotion for my country by any measure or degree. . . . People have been saying that I know nothing of Burmese politics. The trouble is, I know too much. My family knows best how complicated and tricky Burmese politics can be and how much my father had to suffer on this account.

Many who had come to hear the speech out of curiosity left convinced that they now had a leader who would fight for the restoration of democracy in their country. Many ordinary citizens were inspired to join the cause. Many members of the only political party (known as the BSPP) resigned.

Aung San Suu Kyi called for a multiparty election. Instead, on Sunday, September 18, General Saw Maung assumed power in a military takeover of the already military-influenced government. Maung called himself the head of the State Law and Order Council (SLOC) to ensure "peace and tranquility." He said he would allow new political parties to form, but he banned political gatherings. As author Kanbawza Win reported, the military crackdown that followed was carried out "with cold-blooded efficiency. Any crowd in sight was mowed down systematically as the tanks and armored cars rumbled down in perfect formations." It was reported by witnesses that hundreds, perhaps thousands, of Burmese were killed by their own military.

The killings brought the Burmese struggle for democracy to the world's attention. "I would like every country in the world to recognize the fact that the people of Burma are being shot down for no reason at all," Aung San Suu Kyi said in a public statement. Refusing to be intimidated, she participated in the founding of an opposition political party, the National League for Democracy, on September 24, and became its first general secretary. She traveled around Burma, speaking out for democracy despite the government's ban on such activities. When she visited the town of Moulmein, the military through loudspeakers on army trucks, ordered people not to leave their houses; still they flocked to see her.

Always she reminded people that their protest must be nonviolent. "Only if we can control ourselves can we win over our enemies," she said. Author Kanbawza Win suggests, "The spectacle of tens of thousands standing in silence, listening attentively for hours on end to an entirely new message of democracy through discipline, responsibility and nonviolent struggle, must have sent cold shivers down the spine of U Ne Win and his generals."

In the midst of her campaigning, Aung San Suu Kyi saw her mother's

"As long as the struggle for freedom needs to be fought throughout the world, voices such as Aung San Suu Kyi's will summon others to the cause. Whether the cry for freedom comes from central Europe, Russia, Africa, or Asia, it has a common sound: all people must be treated with dignity; all people need to hope."

—Václav Havel, from the foreword of *Freedom from Fear*

health continue to decline. On December 27, 1988, the courageous widow of General Aung San died, and even the military government leaders had to pay their respects to Aung San Suu Kyi in her grief. The funeral on January 2 was attended by hundreds of thousands, but the day passed peacefully. Within weeks Aung San Suu Kyi resumed speaking out for democracy.

By June of 1989 she was challenging the army to end their support of the dictatorship, saying, "My father didn't build up the army in order to oppress the people." On July 20, Michael Aris, who had returned to England, heard the news that his wife had been placed under house arrest. Returning to Burma immediately, he was detained by government officials and told that he could join his wife only if he promised not to make any statements to anyone else while he was there. In other words, he, too, would be under house arrest. Aris responded that he only wanted to be with his wife and their sons. When he was taken to her house, he was relieved to learn that Aung San Suu Kyi was safe, but she had begun a hunger strike to protest the arrest of many of her young supporters. She maintained her hunger strike for 12 days until she was assured that the detainees would not be harmed. On September 2, Aris and the boys returned to England. They would be allowed no contact with her for long periods of time.

It was obvious that the government hoped that cutting Aung San Suu Kyi off from her supporters would mean the end of the democracy movement. But in the 11 months since her first speech, she had made a difference in Burma. She gave the people a taste of freedom from fear. As Kanbawza Win says, "Her invisibility did not leave the Burmese uncertain of what she wanted them to do."

Though she was declared ineligible for election by the government, when the elections were held May 27, 1990, the people voted overwhelmingly for her party, the NLD.

Aung San Suu Kyi dared to tell the world that the government of Burma was shooting down nonviolent demonstrators in the streets. (Courtesy *The Burma Review*)

Although the military's party won only about 2 percent of the vote, they refused to give up control of the government. They continued to harass and arrest members of the NLD.

Though Aung San Suu Kyi could not speak to her family or friends, they continued to speak out for her. In July 1991, the European Parliament awarded her the Sakharov Prize for freedom of thought. Because she would not have been allowed back in to the country if she left to receive the award, she could not be present to accept it.

On October 14, 1991, it was announced that she had won the Nobel Peace Prize for her nonviolent efforts on behalf of human rights in Burma. Czech author and political leader Václav Havel, who nominated her, said, "She is an outstanding example of the power of the powerless." The award was hailed as a victory for the people of Burma, as a declaration that the world had noted their struggle against a brutal regime. Students in Rangoon staged demonstrations on her behalf, and many were arrested. The government forced the NLD to expel Aung San Suu Kyi for having received support from a foreign organization.

On December 10, 1991, dignitaries from around the world gathered in Oslo, Norway, for the awarding of the Nobel Peace Prize. Over 100 Burmese people living in various places around the world were there, but Aung San Suu Kyi, still under house arrest, was not. Her son Myint San Aung accepted the prize for her and

> "I applaud your remarkable courage in pursuing human rights and democracy for the people of Burma. Despite your 4½ years of detention, your determination and courage continue to inspire friends of freedom around the world."
>
> —letter to Aung San Suu Kyi from U.S. President Bill Clinton, February 1994

for "all the men, women and children who . . . continue to sacrifice their well-being, their freedom, and their lives in pursuit of a democratic Burma."

Time passed and Aung San Suu Kyi remained without freedom. Often she did not have enough to eat, and was forced to sell most of her furniture to buy food. She lost weight and suffered a number of nutrition-related health problems. The house in which she was prisoner fell into disrepair and weeds and snakes took over the once-beautiful garden. In February 1993, a group of Nobel Peace Prize laureates assembled in Bangkok to call for her release. In February 1994, a member of the United States Congress visited her and delivered a letter from President Bill Clinton, expressing his support for human rights and democracy in Burma.

Finally, in July 1995, word came that she was no longer under house arrest. Was she truly free, and would conditions improve in Burma? That remained to be seen. "We're nowhere near democracy," she said. "I've been released, that's all." Shortly before a NLD Conference was to be held at Aung San Suu Kyi's home May 26, 1996, the government arrested more than 200 NLD members. The conference went on anyway, although only 18 delegates were able to attend. Some 10,000 supporters gathered outside to protest the government's action. That support, and international pressure, forced the release of some of the NLD members. It is believed that many political prisoners are being subjected to torture and other inhumane treatment. Many of Burma's minorities continue to be repressed.

On August 31, 1995, a video-recorded message from Aung San Suu Kyi opened a meeting of women's groups gathered in China for a world conference on women. "For millennia women have dedicated themselves almost exclusively to the task of nurturing, protecting, and caring for the young and the old," she said, "striving for the conditions of peace that favor life as a whole. It is time to apply in the arena of the world the wisdom and experience that women have gained."

Chronology

June 19, 1945	Aung San Suu Kyi born, Rangoon, Burma
July 19, 1947	her father, General Aung San, is assassinated
January 4, 1948	Burma gains independence from Britain
1960	Aung San Suu Kyi travels to India when her mother becomes ambassador
1962	General Ne Win seizes control of Burmese government in military coup
1964	Aung San Suu Kyi attends college in England
1972	marries Michael Aris
April 1988	travels to Burma to care for her mother
August 26, 1988	makes her first public speech in response to military government's actions against demonstrators
July 19, 1989	placed under house arrest
May 27, 1990	National League for Democracy wins 80 percent of popular vote in free elections; the military refuses to leave power
July 1991	awarded the 1990 Sakharov Prize
December 10, 1991	awarded the Nobel Peace Prize
July 1995	released from house arrest
May 1996	government continues to harass NLD members, disrupting conference at Aung San Suu Kyi's home

Further Reading

Aung San Suu Kyi. *Let's Visit Burma*. London, England: Burke Publishing Co, 1985. A book for young people written by Aung San Suu Kyi. It discusses the history, social fabric, and cultural background of the Burmese people. It is included as a chapter in *Freedom from Fear*.

Aung San Suu Kyi. *Freedom From Fear and Other Writings*. New York: Penguin Books, 1991. A collection of the writings of Aung San Suu Kyi, including thoughts about her father, her country, and speeches made during the democracy movement. Also includes other writings about Aung San Suu Kyi.

Kanbawza Win. *Daw Aung San Suu Kyi, The Nobel Laureate*. Bangkok, Thailand: CPDSK Publications, 1992. Explains the awarding of the Nobel Peace Prize to Aung San Suu Kyi. Includes the acceptance speech given by her son in her absence.

Lintner, Bertil. *Outrage, Burma's Struggle for Democracy*. London, England: White Lotus, 1990. An analysis of the history, politics, and social conditions of Burma, explaining the government resistance movement and Aung San Suu Kyi's involvement. Includes chronology of events between 1987 and 1990.

Rigoberta Menchú has told the story of brutalities she and her family and others experienced in Guatemala. (Courtesy Guatemala Human Rights Commission, photo by Dick Bancroft)

Rigoberta Menchú

QUICHÉ WOMAN OF
GUATEMALA   (1959–)

A small, brown-skinned woman in the colorfully embroidered dress of a Quiché Indian peeked out of a doorway in a small town in Guatemala. The coast appeared to be clear and she stepped out into the street. She hadn't gone far when a speeding car filled with soldiers went past. She knew by their shouts that she had been recognized. Looking around desperately, she saw a little church a short distance away. As the car turned to head back toward her, she quickly ran inside. As her eyes adjusted to the darkened church, Rigoberta Menchú saw that there were only a few people inside. Quickly she moved alongside one of them, and, hoping to disguise herself, she let down her carefully braided long hair and let it fall around her shoulders. She knelt and prayed as the soldiers came barging into the church.

It appeared that her ruse had worked. The soldiers ran through the room and out another door, thinking she had escaped into the marketplace outside. Just to be sure, Menchú waited another hour before quietly leaving the church.

In the meantime, she had plenty to pray about. Soldiers like these killed several members of her family, and the brutal conditions under which Indians were forced to live had killed others. There was no doubt about it.

> She would have to find another place to hide, or it was likely that she too would meet a violent, untimely end.

Rigoberta Menchú was born in 1959 in a small hamlet called Chimel, near Uspantán, in the mountainous province of El Quiché, Guatemala. She is a Quiché Indian, a tribe of the ancient race known as the Maya. Mayan Indians make up well over 50 percent of the population of Guatemala. The rest are either of European or mixed European and Indian descent. People of mixed heritage are known as mestizos or *ladinos*. In general, the Indians of Guatemala, as elsewhere in Central America, are very poor, and are socially, economically, and politically oppressed.

Rigoberta was the sixth of nine children in her family. From the time she was an infant, she was carried down to the *fincas*, the large coastal plantations where coffee, cotton, and sugar are grown. One of her earliest memories is of the truck ride from the mountains to the coast. Into the back of a canvas-covered truck piled about 40 people of all ages, with their assorted dogs, cats, and chickens. During the two-day journey, no one could see anything from the truck so they tried to sleep as much as possible. By the end of the journey, the smell in the back of the stifling truck would be unbearable.

As a young child, Rigoberta helped her mother. "I either picked coffee with her," she wrote in her autobiography, "or looked after my little brother so she could work faster." By the time she was eight, Menchú was working from before dawn to after sundown just to earn little more than a few cents for picking many pounds of coffee. If a coffee branch or cotton plant was damaged in any way, the cost was deducted from her wages. "It's one of the things that taught me to treat things very gently," she says.

Conditions for the Indians who labored in the *fincas* were terrible. They slept on the floor in crowded shacks and got their drinking water from the irrigation ditches that ran along the fields. Many of the Indians became sick from the pesticides that were sprayed on the fields. The oldest Menchú child, Felipe, died from pesticide poisoning before Rigoberta was born. A younger brother, Nicolás, died in 1967 from illness that resulted from malnutrition while the family was working in the *finca*. The family was punished for this tragedy, being forced to leave the plantation without being paid for the days they'd already worked. In the *finca*, Rigoberta says, "Suffering is everywhere." From that moment on, she added, "I was both angry with life and afraid of it, because I told myself, 'This is the life I will lead too; having many children, and having them die.'"

At home in the mountains, the work was still hard, and the people in her village were often cold and wet, but Rigoberta remembers being happier there. There she was taught the traditional ways of her people, to respect herself and all living things. Though the *ladinos*, both in the *fincas* and in the cities, looked down on the Indians, in the native community, everyone was expected to contribute, and thus they were equals.

On her tenth birthday, Rigoberta's mother and father and older brothers and sisters "gave her their experiences." That meant that they told her what they'd learned in their lives to help her. This was how she became an adult. Later, looking back, Rigoberta would say that she had really been an adult all along; she never had the chance to play, be happy, be a child. She never went to school, and never had enough to eat.

Now that she was officially grown up, she had the duty to serve the community in addition to her family responsibilities. She became a catechist, teaching Catholic lessons to the children in her community, and to other groups of children down in the *finca*.

When she was 12, Rigoberta went to work in the home of a wealthy *ladino* family in a big city. She hoped to earn more money for her family and sought a way out of the *finca*. Her employers ridiculed and mistreated her because of their prejudice against Indians. After several months of mistreatment she quit.

Meanwhile, Rigoberta's father had been engaged in the Indians' struggle against the wealthy landowners. Every time the Indians cleared a bit of land and made it productive, rich landowners appeared, claimed the land, and forced the Indians further into the highlands to start over. Vicente Menchú went to the government to complain, and was told that the Indians wouldn't have to leave their land. But the government did nothing to help when the landowners and their armed thugs appeared to claim the Indians' land.

Rigoberta remembered what it was like when the landowners came and dispossessed the people.

> First they went into the houses without permission and got all the people out. Then they went in and threw out all our things. I remember that my mother had her silver necklaces, precious keepsakes from my grandmother, but we never saw them again after that. They stole them all. They threw out our cooking utensils, our earthenware cooking pots. . . . They hurled them in the air, and they hit the ground and broke into pieces. . . . I remember it was pouring rain and we had nothing to protect ourselves from the rain. It took us two days to make a roughly built hut out of leaves.

Her father went on fighting for the community. He knew that what he was doing was dangerous. "If they kill me for trying to defend the land that belongs to us, well, they'll have to kill me," he said. He and his family taught the people to look to the ways of their ancestors to learn how to defend their villages with ambushes and traps. In this way they could make it more difficult for those who would steal their land.

Vicente always asked one of his children to accompany him when he went to see the government officials and the unions so that they could carry on his work if he was killed. Sometimes Rigoberta's brothers went, but often it was Rigoberta.

One day, about the time that Rigoberta left her job as a maid, the landowners had her father arrested for "compromising the sovereignty of the state." For a year the family members worked wherever they could to raise money for lawyers to get him out of prison. During that time, Rigoberta says, "I didn't get home even once. I didn't stop working."

After 14 months, they succeeded in getting Vicente freed. Immediately, he returned to the fight for his people. Within months, he was kidnapped by soldiers, beaten, and left by the side of the road. His friends carried him to town but the landowners had paid the doctors not to treat him; he had to be taken further away by ambulance to be cared for. It was nearly a year before he was able to return home, and even then he was still in pain.

In 1977 Vicente was arrested again, and this time sentenced to life in prison for his political activities. The government called him a Communist and a subversive. But as Rigoberta says, "It wasn't just my father now, it was a whole people behind him. My father was well-known and well-loved in many places so there was a big protest against his arrest." The unions helped, as did priests and nuns. After expensive lawyers were hired, they succeeded in having Vicente released.

In prison Vicente Menchú met a man who suggested that the people unite in a peasants' league to reclaim their lands. Thus the Committee of Peasant Unity, or in Spanish, the Comité de Unidad Campesina (CUC), was formed. Its objectives were to get fair wages and decent treatment for peasant workers, and respect for the Indian culture.

As her father went into hiding to keep from placing his family in greater danger while he carried on his work, Rigoberta and other family members became more involved in his cause. She learned to speak Spanish, the language of the oppressors, so she could deal with them at less of a disadvantage. She also learned several other Indian languages so that she could speak to other villages about getting organized. Most important, from the kindness of several *ladinos* who were sincerely dedicated to the Indians' cause, she learned that not all *ladinos* were bad. It was the powerful and wealthy landlords and the soldiers who were the enemy of the Indians. While most of them were *ladinos*, Rigoberta was learning not to judge by a person's ethnic background, but by his or her actions.

As Rigoberta became more involved in the movement, her father warned her that her enemies might kill her at any time. She said, "I knew that teaching others how to defend themselves against the enemy was a commitment I had to make. I have faith and I believe that happiness belongs to everyone, but that happiness has been stolen by a few. That was what motivated me."

The CUC asked the government to recognize it as a union that defended peasants' rights. The government began arresting CUC leaders, but she went on helping the peasants. When Lucas Garciá, a military leader, came to power in 1978, unspeakable brutalities became more widespread. Reports of rapes, tortures, kidnappings, and massacres flew through the mountains.

As in other Central American countries, there are rebel groups in Guatemala fighting for political change and social reform. These guerrillas tend to hide in the mountains, and ambush government forces. Because this is where the majority of Indian villages are found, the Indians find themselves trapped between the opposing forces. Some Indians have willingly joined the guerrillas, others have been forced to join, or give them food or shelter. For this, the army has staged a war on the Indians that has been labelled genocidal—a deliberate attempt to destroy this ethnic group.

On September 9, 1979, Rigoberta's 16-year-old brother was kidnapped by soldiers as he walked to a nearby village. After being viciously beaten, he was lined up with several others who'd been captured, was doused with gasoline, and burned alive.

On January 31, 1980, Rigoberta's father led a peasant march to the Spanish embassy to protest such atrocities. They hoped to spread the word about human rights abuses in Guatemala. The Spanish ambassador was willing to listen but Guatemalan forces stormed the embassy, setting fires that took the lives of 39 people inside, including embassy workers. The ambassador himself barely managed to escape the flames. Rigoberta's father was one of those who died.

On April 19, 1980, Rigoberta's mother was kidnapped by government troops. After being brutally tortured, she was left to die by a tree.

Such suffering was not unique to the Menchú family. In *The Unfinished Conquest*, author Victor Perera writes, "The Guatemalan army had become the deadliest and most efficient instrument of counter-insurgency in Central America. It also gained a reputation as the most contemptuous of elementary human rights." In *Children of the Maya*, Brent Ashabranner writes,

> By its own count, the army destroyed 440 villages and damaged many others [between 1980 and 1984]. Over thirty thousand Indians were killed. Another 150,000 fled to Mexico and settled in or near refugee camps close to the border; a much smaller number traveled the length of Mexico, mostly on foot, to reach the United States. At least a million more abandoned their villages and sought refuge in the forests and cities of Guatemala.

In 1992 Menchú won the Nobel Peace Prize for her human rights work and in 1993 she became a spokesperson for the United Nations Year of Indigenous Peoples. (UN Photo 182000/M. Grant)

Rigoberta and all of her remaining family members were being hunted by soldiers. They had to stay in hiding. One day she was spotted by soldiers in a little town in Huehuetanango. This was when she hid for an hour in a little church. She then worked for two weeks as a maid in a convent until she was able to get on a plane for Mexico. She hated to leave her country, but it was the only way to stay alive and continue her work.

In Mexico, she met many other Guatemalan refugees, and her commitment to fight for her people grew stronger. She chose to work with the Vicente Menchú Revolutionary Christians, saying, "The work of revolutionary Christians is above all to condemn and denounce the injustices committed against the people."

Rigoberta took advantage of travel opportunities so she could increase awareness of the plight of the Guatemalan refugees. In 1982, she was invited to France to talk about her people; it was there that she told her story to a woman who helped her write her autobiography, *I Rigoberta Menchú.*

In 1987, she helped found the National Committee for Reconciliation, a group that hopes to achieve peaceful negotiations between the Guatemalan government and representatives of opposition groups. The next year she traveled to Guatemala to test the government's claims that things had improved. She and a companion were immediately arrested and charged with "inciting violence."

Rigoberta Menchú now had friends in many places, however, and their telephone calls and telegrams resulted in her speedy release. She immediately held a press conference and bravely spoke of the brutalities that were committed against her family. Author Perera said, "A respectful silence descended over the assemblage. Nothing like this had ever happened in Guatemala before."

In 1992, two previous Nobel Peace Prize winners, Adolfo Pérez Esquivel of Argentina and Desmond Tutu of South Africa, nominated Menchú for the prize. In October, she was informed that she had been selected from 130 candidates to receive the award that year; coincidentally, it was the 500th anniversary of Christopher Columbus' arrival in the "New World." On December 10, 1992, the chairman of the Nobel committee said, "By maintaining a disarming humanity in a brutal world, Rigoberta Menchú appeals to the best in us. She stands as a uniquely potent symbol of a just struggle."

In her acceptance speech, Menchú said, "I consider this prize not as an award to me personally, but rather as one of the great conquests in the struggle for peace, for human rights, and for the rights of indigenous people who, along all the 500 years, have been the victims of genocides, repression, and discrimination."

The president of Guatemala's National Congress was present to applaud Menchú's honor, but other Guatemalan officials were not so happy. In response to her critics,

Rigoberta said that it was all too convenient for those in authority to say

> that the struggles of the Guatemalan people are the work of communists. That crabbed, oversimplified, parochial view has led to people being killed here in the name of communism without anybody understanding what it is.

Menchú used the $1.2 million award to establish the Rigoberta Menchú Tum Foundation to work for human rights for the indigenous people of Central America, particularly of Guatemala. In 1993, she was asked to serve as the goodwill ambassador for the United Nations Year of Indigenous Peoples. On June 6 of that year, Ramiro de León Carpio, a human rights activist, became president of Guatemala. It was part of the movement within Guatemala toward peace that culminated in the last days of December 1996 with the signing of a peace treaty that ended the 36-year-old civil war in that country. Some of the many thousands who had fled Guatemala during the conflict between the government and the guerrillas prepared to return. Alvaro Arzu, who had been elected president of Guatemala earlier in 1996, said, "Today we begin a new phase, but there is much to be done." During the celebration, Rigobert Menchú said, "This fiesta should be extended to all corners of Latin America, carrying the message that a political solution can be found to conflict." Only time would tell if this season of hope would bring real change to the oppressed people of Guatemala.

Chronology

1959	Rigoberta Menchú is born, Chimel, Guatemala

1967	a younger brother dies of malnutrition
1972	Rigoberta's father Vicente arrested; Rigoberta works to earn money for lawyers
1977	Vicente Menchú arrested again; helps form CUC, peasant union
1978	government actions against Indians escalates
September 1979	Rigoberta's brother killed by soldiers
January 31, 1980	Rigoberta's father dies in Spanish embassy fire
April 1980	Rigoberta's mother killed by soldiers
1981	Rigoberta escapes to Mexico
1983	autobiography published
December 1992	awarded the Nobel Peace Prize
1993	serves as goodwill ambassador for United Nations Year of Indigenous Peoples
December 1996	peace treaty signed between the Guatemalan government and guerrillas, ending 36 years of civil war

Further Reading

Ashabranner, Brent. *Children of the Maya, A Guatemalan Indian Odyssey*. New York: Dodd Mead, 1986. Tells the story of Guatemalans of Mayan descent who fled the violence in their homeland for refugee camps in Mexico and found a new home in Florida. It is written for young people.

Lazo, Caroline. *Rigoberta Menchú*. New York: Dillon Press, 1994. A biography of Rigoberta Menchú written for young people after she was awarded the Nobel Peace Prize.

Menchú, Rigoberta. *I Rigoberta Menchú, an Indian Woman in Guatemala*. Ed. and introduced by Elisabeth Burgos-Debray. New York: Verso, 1984. Rigoberta Menchú's autobiography. Contains heartbreaking descriptions of the difficult life of native Guatemalans, and a bloodcurdling account of atrocities committed by the military.

Perera, Victor. *Unfinished Conquest, The Guatemalan Tragedy*. Berkeley: University of California Press, 1993. Traces the modern history of Guatemala through military juntas and peasant labor movements. Includes some information on Rigoberta Menchú more recent than her autobiography.

Trout, Lawana Hooper. *The Maya*. New York: Chelsea House, 1991. Examines the history of the Maya Indians of Mexico and Central America. Includes information on the current situation for these people. Written for young people.

Index

This index is designed as an aid to access the narrative text and special features. **Boldface** numbers indicate main headings. *Italic* numbers indicate illustrations. The letter *c* following a page number refers to an entry in the chronology.